DUNHAM MASSEY

Cheshire

THE NATIONAL TRUST

Dunham Massey lies three miles south-west of Altrincham off A56; junction 19 off M6.

Acknowledgements

This guidebook draws on the previous edition, written by Gervase Jackson-Stops and Merlin Waterson in 1981 and revised by Belinda Cousens in 1991. It is heavily indebted to the extensive research undertaken by them and by many others, including, most recently, David Eastwood, Siân Miller and Dr Pamela Sambrook. Access to the family papers has been greatly improved thanks to the comprehensive cataloguing of the Dunham archive by John Hodgson, and of the Enville archive by Sandy Haynes. The garden section owes much to John Sales, the National Trust's former Head of Gardens, and the picture entries are based on the work of St John Gore and Alastair Laing, former and present pictures advisers to the National Trust.

The late Lord Stamford's nephews and niece, John and Oliver Turnbull and Marjorie Williams, have been unfailingly supportive and have provided useful information about Dunham's recent history. So too has Arthur Shufflebotham, who worked on the estate from 1935 to 1985, and Peter Chapman, agent to Lord Stamford and subsequently to the National Trust. At Dunham, I have received help from all, but I must mention in particular Margaret Stone, the Collections Manager. It is her exemplary care which ensures that the house is always seen at its best. Finally, my biggest debt of gratitude is to Jenny Phimister, who typed the manuscript and has overcome the not inconsiderable hurdle of my handwriting.

James Rothwell

Photographs: Courtauld Institute of Art p. 53; National Trust pp. 6, 10, 37 (top), 44 (top left), 60, 61; NT/Robert Thrift pp. 23 (top), 50, 62 (top left); National Trust Photographic Library p. 59 (top right); NTPL/Matthew Antrobus pp. 7, 8, 41 (top and bottom); NTPL/Neil Campbell-Sharp pp. 46, 47; NTPL/Andreas von Einsiedel pp. 13, 14, 15, 16, 17, 18, 21, 25, 33, 34, 37 (bottom), 38; NTPL/John Hammond front cover, pp. 4, 9, 23 (bottom), 25, 26, 28, 56, 59 (bottom left), back cover; NTPL/Angelo Hornak pp. 5, 42, 43, 49; NTPL/Fraser Marr p. 57 (bottom left and right); NTPL/Nick Meers pp. 44–5; NTPL/Brenda Norrish p. 19; NTPL/Mike Williams pp. 1, 32, 48, 51, 52, 54, 57 (top), 62 (bottom right), 63, 64.

If you would like to become a member or make a donation, please telephone 0844 800 1895 (minicom 0844 800 4410); write to The National Trust, PO Box 39, Warrington WA5 7WD; or see our website at www.nationaltrust.org.uk

Typeset from disc and designed by James Shurmer (9 08)

Printed by Hawthornes for National Trust (Enterprises) Ltd, Heelis, Kemble Drive, Swindon, Wilts SN2 2NA on stock made from 75% recycled fibre

Bibliography

The Dunham Massey Papers have been deposited, as the late Lord Stamford requested, in the John Rylands University Library of Manchester. A full catalogue has been produced.

AXON, Ernest, 'The Family Bothe and the Church in the 15th and 16th Centuries', *Transactions of the Lancashire and Cheshire Antiquarian Society*, liii, 1939, pp. 32ff; BECKETT, J.V., and C. Jones, *Financial Improvidence and Political Independence in the early Eighteenth Century: George Booth, 2nd Earl of Warrington (1675–1758)*, 1982; BEEVERS, D., 'Percy Macquoid, Artist Decorator and Historian', *Antique Collector*, vi, vii, 1984; COMPTON HALL, J., *Dunham Massey: An Account of its History including a brief Description of the Recent Restoration*, 1909 (unpublished); GORE, St John, 'Portraits and the Grand Tour', *Apollo*, July 1978, pp. 24–31; GREEN, Pippa, *The History of the Garden at Dunham Massey*, 1983 (unpublished thesis); HARDY, John, and Gervase Jackson-Stops, 'The Second Earl of Warrington and the "Age of Walnut"', *Apollo*, July 1978, pp. 12–23; HARRIS, John, 'A Bird's-eye View of Dunham Massey', *Apollo*, July 1978, pp. 4–11; HAYWARD, J.F., 'The Earl of Warrington's Plate', *Apollo*, July 1978, pp. 32–9; HODGSON, John, 'The Dunham Massey Papers', *Transactions of the Lancashire and Cheshire Antiquarian Society*, xci, 1995; JACKSON-STOPS, Gervase, 'Dunham Massey', *Country Life*, 4 June, 11 June, 2 July, 9 July 1981, pp. 1562, 1664, 18, 106; JONES, J.R., *Booth's Rising of 1659*, 1957; JONES, J.R., *William, Earl of Stamford, 1850–1910*, n.d. (privately printed); LAING, Alastair, 'Sensible, Sincere Creatures', *Country Life*, 8 February 1990, pp. 62–5; LEACH, H.J., *Tales & Sketches of Old Bowdon & Altrincham*, 1880; LOMAX, J. and J. Rothwell, *Country House Silver from Dunham Massey*, 2006; MacANDREW, Donald, 'Equestrienne', *The Saturday Book Review*, 1960s; MILLER, Siân, 'The Emperor's Room at Dunham Massey', *Apollo*, April 1999, pp. 50–3; MORRISON, Jane, 'Macquoid at Dunham Massey', *Country Life*, 2 July 1987, pp. 156–60; ROTHWELL, James, 'The re-assembly of the Warrington silver at Dunham Massey, Cheshire', *Apollo*, April 2001, pp. 30–4; SALES, John, 'A Quality Unsurpassed', *Country Life*, 9 June 1994, pp. 112–15; SAMBROOK, P., *A Country House at Work, Three Centuries of Dunham Massey*, 2003; SWARBRICK, John, 'Dunham Massey Hall', *Transactions of the Lancashire and Cheshire Antiquarian Society*, xlii, 1925, pp. 53ff; WILKIE, C., *The Lives of Sir George and Henry Booth, First and Second Baron Delamer, of Dunham Massey* (unpublished thesis); WOODSIDE, Robert, *Archaeological Survey of the Dunham Massey Estate*, 1998 (unpublished).

(*Front cover*) Decorative base of one of the columns on the exterior of Dunham Massey

(*Back cover*) Long line of servants' bells in the corridor next to the Still Room

(*Title-page*) The coat of arms of the 2nd Earl of Warrington (Study Ante-Room)

CONTENTS

DUNHAM MASSEY

Tranquillity and Turbulence

In spite of its proximity to Manchester, Dunham Massey is a place of tranquillity, a retreat from the bustle of everyday life. The open fields and woodland of the estate act as a buffer for the ancient, walled deer-park, with the great red-brick house at its centre, lying low and solid next to the remains of the moat which protected its forerunners.

The house is comparatively plain, reflecting the simplicity of taste and the determination to avoid public life of George Booth, 2nd Earl of Warrington, for whom it was built in the first half of the 18th century. Lord Warrington was reacting against the near-ruinous involvement of his father and grandfather in the turbulent politics of the 17th century. He had been particularly affected by seeing his father reduced to weeping 'from the greatness of his debts', and he was determined that his heirs should enjoy the status and financial security which he had come close to losing. Everything he did – his loveless marriage to an heiress, the building of a new house on the foundations of the old, the investment in a vast quantity of new silver, and the planting of 100,000 trees – was either an affirmation of the family's ancestry and long links with Dunham, or an act of financial prudence.

On Lord Warrington's death in 1758, the estate passed in sound heart to the Greys, Earls of Stamford, who managed it with equal care. They had tasted national fame at a far higher level than the Booths and had suffered even worse. When the Greys had tried to set Lady Jane Grey on the throne in 1553, three members of the family, including the

(Opposite page) Dunham Massey from the north in 1751 – one of the famous series of bird's-eye views by John Harris (Great Gallery). It shows the house and landscape created by the 2nd Earl of Warrington

The 2nd Earl of Warrington's Dutch mastiff, Old Vertue, painted around 1700, probably by Jan Wyck (Great Gallery). In the background is the house before it was rebuilt by the 2nd Earl

innocent sixteen-year-old herself, lost their lives. Estates and titles were also lost, and a foray into the politics of the Civil War served only to reaffirm the prudence of a quieter life. The 4th, 5th and 6th Earls were content to hover on the edge of prominence and to consolidate their already enviable wealth. They treated Dunham with the greatest respect, guarding the estate against the encroachment of industrial Manchester. It was this careful tenure that ensured the remarkable survival of Lord Warrington's formal park, with its seven radiating avenues, as well as his collections of paintings, furniture and silver.

The 7th Earl, who succeeded in 1845, was a less careful figure. His fondness for horses, his massive gardening schemes and his gambling might have led to greater change, but he died in middle age, before managing to dissipate his entire fortune. Cheshire society snubbed his second wife, Catherine Cocks, who had been a circus performer in her youth, and this is said to have encouraged him to abandon Dunham for his Staffordshire estate at Enville,

taking all the silver and the best of the pictures with him. The house was let, and estate land on the edge of Altrincham was developed to provide villas for the prosperous merchants of Manchester.

On the death of the Countess in 1905, the estates were split, and Dunham alone passed to William Grey, 9th Earl of Stamford (his uncle, the 8th Earl, had predeceased the Countess). He and his wife, Penelope Theobald, renovated and redecorated the house, and it is largely the schemes introduced for them by the furniture historian Percy Macquoid that you can see today. What remained of the historic collection was carefully incorporated, but much had been lost, and it was not until the 1920s, with a series of sales from the family's other houses, that the 10th and last Earl of Stamford was able to begin returning paintings and silver to Dunham Massey. He ensured that the estate was in good heart when it passed to the National Trust after his death in 1976. Lord Stamford's bequest was one of the most generous ever made to the National Trust.

TOUR OF THE HOUSE

The Exterior

THE APPROACH AND SOUTH LAWN

A sweeping avenue of small-leaf limes planted in the early 20th century marks the approach to Dunham Massey from the north. The drive continues along the edge of the moat, which was traditionally said to be associated with a Norman castle. At this point, you can see the house and its service buildings, picturesquely grouped beyond the water. The lawns and lush plantings of the garden stretch out on one side, and, on the other, the gold-topped cupola of the coach-house rises above the long rear walls of the stable buildings.

Today you pass through the coach-house arch to reach the house, but the drive continues on for another 100 metres before swinging sharply to the left and converging with four other drives coming from different directions. This is the 18th-century arrangement, which ensured that all those approaching Dunham Massey would see the principal façade square on, at the end of an open forecourt now known as the south lawn. This took the place of a walled and gated mid-17th-century enclosure as part of the 2nd Earl of Warrington's comprehensive landscape scheme. His tight, triple rows of limes, kept pollarded to retain their shape, were reintroduced in the 1980s, and the commanding early 18th-century lead lions representing the Booth crest still stand on their massive stone plinths. The lead statue of a Moor from North Africa supporting a sundial is also still in place before the front door. It was almost certainly supplied by John Van Nost or his assistant, Andries Carpentière, the latter being responsible for monuments to the 2nd Earl's brothers and parents in St Mary's church, Bowdon. The low stone walls and three of the four urn-topped piers flanking the south front

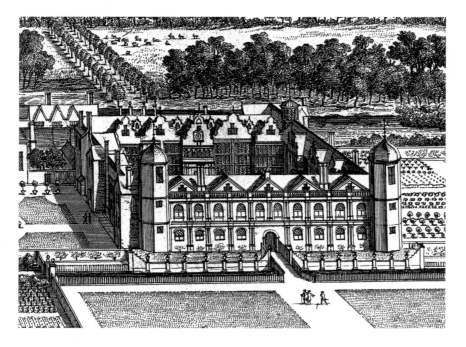

(Left)
Kip and Knyff's 1697 bird's-eye view shows the south range as rebuilt by 'Young' Sir George Booth, probably in the 1650s

(Right)
The south front today

were, however, done away with in 1789–90 by the 5th Earl of Stamford, when he naturalised the landscape immediately around the house. The obelisks which marked the entrance to the south lawn were reduced to the present squat piers in the mid-19th century, and the drive layout is Edwardian, re-establishing the formal approach done away with in the late 18th century.

THE SOUTH FRONT

According to Sir Peter Leycester, writing in 1673, 'Young' Sir George Booth, 2nd Baronet (later 1st Lord Delamer) added the south range, probably in the 1650s, thereby linking the pre-existing west and east ranges and enclosing the courtyard. In the 1730s John Norris was brought in to rebuild the entire house by the 2nd Earl of Warrington. He designed a severe façade of brick accentuated by pairs of bays breaking forward slightly on either side and an essentially unornamented stone centrepiece.

The thin, strip-like windows of the centrepiece and the old-fashioned mullions and transoms at ground-floor level were quite unlike anything else done at the time, but they were unfortunately done away with in 1789–90 by John Hope of Liverpool for Lord Warrington's grandson, the 5th Earl of

Stamford, in an attempt to make the façade more conventional. The result was rather monotonous and barracks-like, and it fell to the architect Joseph Compton Hall to restore balance to the façade as part of his overhaul of the whole house between 1905 and 1908. Compton Hall lowered the roof-line between the projecting bays, replacing the attic windows with pedimented dormer windows, introduced a stronger cornice and embellished the centrepiece. The Greys' motto, *A ma puissance* ('To the upmost of my power'), is carved in bold relief above the entrance door, for which Compton Hall retained the early 18th-century wrought-iron screen.

The east and north fronts, described below, can be seen from the garden.

THE EAST FRONT

Norris's east front remained intact until 1822, when John Shaw created a new dining room (now the Saloon) for the 6th Earl of Stamford. This entailed the rebuilding of the centre of the range and the addition of a semicircular bay. Plate glass was introduced into the first-floor windows in 1855–6, when the rooms behind were refurbished for the 7th

The north front

Earl's second countess. In 1908 Compton Hall, who had initially proposed making this the entrance front, altered the stone steps which give access to the garden. The balustrades incorporate elements of the ironwork removed by Shaw from the north front and probably supplied by the great Derbyshire ironsmith Robert Bakewell in 1735.

THE NORTH FRONT

This long, low and very plain façade is much as it was when first built for Lord Warrington in the 1730s. The most significant change has been the loss of all but four of the original thick-barred sash-windows on the ground floor and all but three on the first floor. Most of the rest were replaced with finer, fewer-paned versions as part of John Hope's alteration of the Great Gallery in 1783–4 and John Shaw's work of the 1820s. Compton Hall replaced the windows of the Great Gallery again in the early 20th century, reverting to more sympathetic proportions, and also added the stone-clad single-storey bay and tall windows on the ground floor to light his new dining room. The open, pyramidal steps introduced by Shaw were replaced at the same time by a flanking set, more akin to the original, but

with a stone, rather than an iron, balustrade at the request of Lord and Lady Stamford. A simple centrepiece was created incorporating the motto of the Countess's family, the Theobalds – *Benigno numine* ('Under benign influence') – and the 9th Earl and Countess's intertwined initials.

The two courtyards of the house are described below, as they occur in the tour.

The Interior

THE ENTRANCE HALL

An entrance passage existed here from the mid-17th century, when the south range was added for the 1st Lord Delamer. It served only to give access to the Inner Courtyard, from which the Great Hall could be approached. When the 2nd Earl of Warrington rebuilt the house in the 1730s, he retained this inconvenient and outmoded arrangement, probably because of his extreme conservatism and in order to save money.

It was for the 9th Earl and Countess of Stamford that Compton Hall created something more fitting by incorporating two flanking rooms. He maintained an atmosphere of intimacy and comfort, something which pervades most of the interiors at Dunham, by not overexpanding the space and by liberal use of polished oak.

DECORATION

The rest of the decoration was entrusted to Percy Macquoid, an interior designer and furniture historian who was married to Lady Stamford's cousin and who was brought in to advise on the finishing of the house in April 1907. In close liaison with Lady Stamford, he chose the rich red paper, which survives, blending harmoniously with the oak and softening the impact of the stone floor. It was supplied and installed by the fashionable London decorators Morant & Co. in September 1907.

PICTURES

To the right of the fireplace is a framed copy of a *memorial poem* to the 6th Earl of Stamford, who died in 1845. In the bay opposite the fireplace is the *illuminated address* presented by the tenantry of the Cheshire estates to the 9th Earl of Stamford on his official return to Dunham Massey with his family on 8 August 1906. The Homecoming, as the event became known, occurred almost exactly 50 years after the 7th Earl had abandoned the house and was met by genuine enthusiasm in the locality. A carriage procession from the station at Hale halted at Altrincham and proceeded through the estate, ending on the south lawn where the address was presented by William Davies, the oldest tenant on the estate.

FURNITURE

The furniture is mostly of oak. The large *gate-leg table* in front of the fireplace, the *side-table* beneath the illuminated address, and the *oak coffer* to its right are all 18th-century. The *walnut-framed mirror* above the coffer is late 17th-century. The *mahogany and oak longcase clock* is by Benjamin Peers of Chester, 1810. The *late 18th-century mahogany stick barometer* to the left of the fireplace has an action by E. Scarlet.

CERAMICS

ON MANTELSHELF:

Chinese blue-and-white octagonal tureen and cover, Qianlong (1736–95).

Two Chinese blue-and-white Yanyan vases, both Kangxi (1662–1722).

LADY STAMFORD'S PARLOUR

Under Compton Hall's final scheme, which had developed by early 1906, the ground floor of the south range was given over to the private day rooms of the 9th Earl and Countess. Lady Stamford's Parlour was where she would write letters and deal with household matters, often standing by the window to gain better light than could be had from the low-voltage electrical system which had been installed in 1906. It also served as her sitting room, particularly after the adjoining Chintz Drawing Room (not open) had fallen out of use, and it was here in later years that her grandchildren greeted her, on arriving for their annual summer visit to Dunham. Then as now, the room was crowded, reflecting Lady Stamford's busy, but ordered, life. There were piles of books and magazines, copies of the *Daily Mail* (which Lady Stamford took for Ann Temple's problem page), little balls of string, folded brown paper saved from incoming parcels, and other assorted oddments. Photographs of her parents, children, grandchildren and siblings sit on the bookcases, and nearly all the pictures here relate in some way to her life.

Lady Stamford and her children, by J. Ernest Breun

Casualties convalescing in the Inner Courtyard during the First World War, when Dunham served as a hospital. Lady Jane Grey is in the centre of the group, seated on the steps

Amongst them, and on the mantelshelf, are a number of moralistic poems and mottoes, indicative of the indefatigable character which enabled Lady Stamford to cope with managing the estate after her husband died in 1910.

This evocative room appears now much as it did in 1959, when the Countess died at the age of 93.

FURNITURE

The little walnut chest-of-drawers to the left of the fireplace is Italian, 18th-century. Lady Stamford's *desk, the pair of chairs* (part of a larger set) opposite the entrance door with delicately carved Gothic splat-backs, and the *two open armchairs* are all mahogany and late 18th-century.

THE INNER COURTYARD

George Booth, 2nd Earl of Warrington reconstructed the courtyard in the mid-1730s, and his gilded cipher, the intertwined initials 'GW' beneath an earl's coronet, can be seen on the rainwater heads. The tall, narrow windows of the north range, which contains the Great Hall, have old-fashioned stone mullions and transoms, which were probably a deliberate echo of the earlier house. Mullions and transoms extend around the ground floor of the west and south ranges, and the treatment of the latter, with its plain parapet, stone centrepiece and three tiers of unaltered windows, is very like that of the original south front.

In 1823 John Shaw constructed across the courtyard a covered passage which survived into the early 20th century and was, according to the 9th Earl's daughter, Lady Jane Turnbull, who saw it as a child, particularly dark and oppressive. The passage was removed by Compton Hall, who embellished the stonework of the two facing centrepieces, thereby unfortunately impairing the careful balance of what are otherwise sparsely decorated façades.

His layout of the yard itself is considerably more successful, its central fountain with walks around being inspired by Hampton Court.

PLANTING

The courtyard parterre contains herbaceous plants in shades of blue, yellow and white, and light foliage. Scented climbers cover the walls, including on the north wall *Actinidia* and various cultivars of *Clematis viticella*.

On returning to the Entrance Hall, turn immediately left.

THE SOUTH CORRIDOR AND CRIMSON STAIRCASE

For the new approach to the principal reception rooms, avoiding the courtyard, Compton Hall used the eastern half of the stone-flagged South Corridor, moving the bottom flight of the Crimson Stairs over to the Inner Courtyard wall to give more space and greater light and opening up a doorway into the Saloon. Percy Macquoid continued the decoration through from the Entrance Hall and introduced the tapestry curtains, which were supplied by Morant & Co. in 1907. The Trust repaired the wallpaper in 1981, using end-rolls that had been carefully stored away after the Edwardian redecoration was completed.

The Crimson Staircase, originally linking the three floors of bedrooms which made up the south range, is one of five secondary staircases in the main body of the house, all of which are early 18th-century and constructed of oak.

PICTURES

SOUTH CORRIDOR:

The portraits on the window wall include *Lady Diana Cecil*, daughter and co-heiress of the 2nd Earl of Exeter, and her second husband, *Thomas Bruce, 1st Earl of Elgin*. Lady Diana's sister, Lady Anne Cecil, married the 1st Earl of Stamford. Opposite is *'Old' Sir George Booth, 1st Bt*, the builder of Elizabethan and Jacobean Dunham. To his right are two paintings of hunters which probably belonged to the 5th Earl of Stamford. They were painted by Daniel Clowes, who was much patronised by the gentry of the North-West. The black and gold frames here and elsewhere in the house were first introduced in the early 18th century by the 2nd Earl of Warrington.

FOOT OF CRIMSON STAIRCASE:

JOHN KIP (d. 1722) after LEONARD KNYFF (1650–1721)
Dunham Massey from the South, 1697
The house, garden and park are shown as they were just after the 2nd Earl of Warrington had inherited, at the start of his massive campaign of planting (note the young trees in avenues to the north and south of the house) and before he embarked upon rebuilding. All of the buildings depicted have gone, with the exception of the early 17th-century mill to the left of the walled forecourt.

After (?) Sir PETER LELY (1618–80)
'Young' Sir George Booth, 1st Lord Delamer (1622–84)
The grandson and successor of 'Old' Sir George, he was imprisoned for his part in the Royalist rising of 1659. He was released in 1660 and created Baron Delamer by Charles II in 1661. His second wife was Lady Elizabeth Grey, daughter of the 1st Earl of Stamford.

Sir GODFREY KNELLER (1646/9–1723)
Henry Booth, 1st Earl of Warrington (1652–94)
Twice imprisoned in the Tower of London for his opposition to the Catholic James II. For his subsequent support of the Glorious Revolution, William III created him Earl in 1690. He soon lost favour, retired to Dunham and died at the age of 42, disappointed and nearly bankrupt.

PHOTOGRAPHS

On the side-tables in the South Corridor are studio portraits of the 9th Earl and Countess of Stamford, in their robes for the coronation of Edward VII in 1902.

FURNITURE

SOUTH CORRIDOR:

Pair of marble-topped mahogany side-tables, English, *c*.1720.

A carved and grained bench, c.1695. One of a series of ornately carved benches probably introduced by the 6th Earl of Stamford in the 1820s.

FOOT OF CRIMSON STAIRCASE:

A carved walnut bench, c.1695, of Dutch influence but probably English-made. In the central oval medallion is an elegantly carved monogram.

Eight-day English striking spring clock in a mahogany case, *c.1840.*

METALWORK

SOUTH CORRIDOR:

A bronze circular bowl on a tripod stand of winged mythical beasts, *c.1815,* 'cast from the cannon taken at the battle of Waterloo'.

SOUTH CORRIDOR AND CRIMSON STAIRS:

Four gilt-bronze hanging lamps, c.1830, made for colza oil. They were adapted for gas, probably in the 1860s, then moved here from elsewhere in the house and electrified in 1907.

THE SALOON

It was here in the years immediately before and after the First World War, when Lady Stamford hosted house parties at Dunham, that the family and their guests would gather before dinner and reassemble afterwards to be entertained. There would sometimes be dancing, with the furniture moved aside and carpets rolled up. Lady Jane Turnbull recalled playing games such as Up Jenkins, Dumb Crambo and Charades: 'We didn't have the serious conversations or high-powered Bridge. There was nothing like that ... we were [the young people] all, all so happy ... so lighthearted compared to the present day.'

During the First World War, when Dunham became a military hospital, the Saloon was filled with iron beds in order to serve as the chief ward. By the late 1930s, when entertaining on the grand scale had ceased at Dunham, the Saloon served primarily as an impressive gallery by which to reach the rest of the house, and as a suitable display space for the best of the late 18th-century portraits.

The 2nd Earl of Warrington's Great Parlour and Withdrawing Room originally filled this space, leading off the high end of the Great Hall in a conventional late medieval or Tudor manner. The arrangement probably replicated that of 'Old' Sir George Booth's house and survived until 1822, when the two rooms were amalgamated by John

Shaw for the 6th Earl of Stamford, in order to create a larger dining room. Shaw raised the ceiling by about three feet, decorated it with the guilloche-patterned bands which can still be seen and also added the semicircular bay with its screen of scagliola (imitation marble) columns, and re-used the massive marble fireplace. The elaborate gilt pelmets were introduced at the same time.

The room must have been thoroughly inconvenient, as it was 160 feet from the Kitchen, and food had to be brought across the Great Hall. Compton Hall pointed out to the 9th Earl that a mere 'cutlet would get almost cold in transit', and in his 1905 report he recommended that a new dining room should be created adjacent to the Kitchen. He wished the vacated space to be used for the entrance to the house, but this was overruled because of the loss of privacy to the garden which would have resulted, and instead a drawing room was created, to be known as the Saloon.

DECORATION

Much to his annoyance, Compton Hall was not entrusted with the decoration of this room. Instead, Percy Macquoid chose the strong green of the walls, 'a green considerably deeper than duck-egg', as he wrote in July 1905, and added the deep anthemion (honeysuckle) frieze. Macquoid was also responsible for the yellow silk damask of the curtains, which were rewoven in 1980; for the reupholstery of the early 18th-century walnut chairs; and for the dying of the Donegal carpets moss-green. On his advice, most of the textiles, in yellows, greens and tans, were supplied by Morant & Co., making the room an unusually complete and rare example of the work of the finest Edwardian decorators and upholsterers. Macquoid himself wrote of it to Lady Stamford in September 1908: 'You really allowed me to persuade you and very kindly believed in me. I think it is a rare combination and should now be a strange room into which red must never enter, even on the dresses of them that inhabit it.'

PICTURES

The cream of the picture collection was removed by the 7th Earl of Stamford to Enville Hall in Staffordshire from the late 1850s and remained there when the family's estates were split in 1905. It was not until Enville's pictures were dispersed at two great sales in 1928 and 1931 that the 10th

The Saloon

Earl of Stamford was able to secure some of those which had previously been at Dunham, together with others which he deemed to be important because they depicted members of the family. He subsequently rehung the whole house, choosing to gather together in the Saloon the late 18th-century portraits, many of which had been here before they were taken to Enville. Lord Stamford's arrangement, which sits so comfortably with the Edwardian decoration, survives essentially unaltered.

To the right of the entrance door and dominating the room which he created is a full-length portrait by George Romney of the *6th Earl of Stamford,* for which he sat in 1790, when he was 25. The 6th Earl, who was fondly remembered by his tenants as an 'old-fashioned kind-hearted country gentleman', is also depicted at the age of eight in the portrait by James Shaw hanging at the left-hand end of the fireplace wall. Either side of the fireplace are three-quarter-lengths of his parents, *the 5th Earl* and *Countess of Stamford,* by Romney, to whom they also sat in 1790. To the right of the 5th Earl is Lady Stamford's brother *William Henry, 3rd Duke of Portland,* who was twice Prime Minister. The portrait is a copy of a Reynolds at Welbeck Abbey in Nottinghamshire and was painted by John Powell, one of Reynolds's assistants.

Within the bay, *the 5th Earl,* by Francis Cotes, and his *Countess* by Benjamin West, are depicted in their youth, and between them are their second and third sons, *the Hon. William Booth Grey* and *the Hon. and Rev. Anchitel Grey,* both by John Halls. Another portrait of *Anchitel Grey*, by Romney, hangs to the left of the full-length of his brother, *the 6th Earl*, whilst to the right is their youngest brother, *the Hon. Henry Grey*, attributed to William Beechey. Henry, a naval captain, died in the shipwreck of the *Weasel* in Barnstaple Bay in 1799, aged 24.

PHOTOGRAPHS

On the chests-of-drawers are signed photographs of Emperor Haile Selassie of Ethiopia, his son the Crown Prince, and Princess Mary, the Princess Royal, all of whom visited Dunham between the wars. The fourth photograph shows the 10th Earl as a child in his court clothes.

FURNITURE

The furniture for the Saloon was selected by Macquoid, who either picked out pieces from other rooms or recommended the purchase of specific items. In the latter category are the *longcase clock* of about 1750 by John Kirby of Bromley in Kent and the early 18th-century *six-leaf screen*, both of which are black-lacquered with gilt decoration in the oriental manner.

The early 18th-century *walnut seat furniture* was acquired by the 2nd Earl of Warrington. It was reupholstered in the current tan cut-velvet by Morant & Co. in 1908. Other furniture likely to have been acquired by Lord Warrington includes the large *gilt pier-glass* at the far end of the room and the late 17th-century *side-table* to the right of the entrance door with its exuberant marquetry decoration of flowers and foliage.

The satinwood bookcases, similar to designs by Gillows of Lancaster, were bought by the 5th Earl of Stamford and date from about 1790. They were in the Great Gallery in 1819 and were moved here from elsewhere in the house by Macquoid, after being repaired and re-polished by Morant & Co. Lady Stamford wrote to Macquoid in September 1908: 'The satinwood cabinets are in their places and look extremely well ... and we are *very* pleased.'

The small marquetry *bonheur-du-jour* (lady's writing-table), with ormolu (gilt bronze) mounts of

(Right) The satinwood bookcases in the Saloon were probably bought new by the 5th Earl of Stamford around 1790. Percy Macquoid had them repaired and moved to this room

c.1770, in the bay is in the style of the royal cabinet-maker John Cobb.

CERAMICS

FLANKING FIREPLACE:

Pair of Chinese vases with trumpet necks and k'uei dragon handles, Dao Guang, c.1820–30, on mahogany stands.

LIGHT-FITTINGS

The large cut-glass chandelier by F.&C. Osler of Birmingham, c.1850, was moved here from the Great Gallery by Macquoid. He added the other fittings, stating that otherwise 'you will never be able to see the pictures at night'. He apologised for the placing of the light switches, which Lady Stamford considered too prominent, adding, 'There is nothing more serious in taste ... a nice room is often spoilt by unsuitable fittings.'

THE GREAT HALL

The Great Hall had a particular potency for the family, because it was here on 14 September 1682 that Charles II's illegitimate son, the Duke of Monmouth, who was trying to promote himself as heir to the throne, 'sat at meat', and, according to a contemporary account, 'the doors were set open and the rabble suffered not only to gaze into the room but to come in and view the Duke, entering at one door and going out at another'. So, when the 2nd Earl of Warrington reconstructed the Great Hall in the 1730s, it was entirely in keeping with his conservative attitude that he should retain its original site and probably its original proportions.

The 2nd Earl evoked the former appearance of the room by using mullions and transoms in the tall windows, but he did not reuse any of the old fittings, and nothing now survives of the screens passage which must have run along the far end of the room. In its new, 18th-century guise, the Great Hall was exceptionally austere, the only decoration being its carved stone overmantel. This was almost certainly designed by the obscure but highly sophisticated Monsieur Boujet, who is reputed to have designed Montagu House in London and who provided Lord Warrington with drawings for overmantels in the 1690s. Boujet (a Huguenot, and so a Protestant, which would have suited Lord Warrington) was heavily influenced by the engravings of the designer Daniel Marot. Given that the style of the overmantel would have been very outdated by the 1730s, it may have been made for the old house and set up here on a later fire-surround as part of the rebuilding.

DECORATION

The 9th Earl and Countess were equally conscious of the room's historic importance and were initially anxious to avoid any fundamental change. However, structural repairs meant that redecoration was inevitable. Macquoid advised that 'the character of the house is its interest and that is of the 2nd half of the 17th century & onward'. So for his embellishment of the plasterwork on the upper walls and ceiling, he drew on three of the most famous of 17th-century buildings: Inigo Jones's Banqueting House in Whitehall, Wilton House near Salisbury, and Sir Roger Pratt's Coleshill House in Oxfordshire. For the plaster frame above the fireplace, he adopted the early

The Great Hall overmantel is decorated with the coat of arms and boar supporters of the 2nd Earl of Warrington

18th-century style of William Kent. He retained Lord Warrington's panelling, but he embellished the overdoors to fit in with the plasterwork, 'scraping and recolouring it and using it as a key note in the decoration', as he proposed in March 1907. He had the walls above painted their current yellow, which was carefully washed in 1979, when the stone colour of the ceiling and frieze was renewed, and the damask curtains were rewoven.

PICTURES

In designing the plasterwork for the upper walls, Macquoid probably intended to incorporate the copies of Titian's *The Vendramin Family* and Rubens's *Pythian Apollo*, together with Thomas Stringer's two paintings of the 5th Earl's Harlequin Great Dane, *Turpin*. All four had been in the room since at least 1787, but when it came to rehanging in October 1907, Macquoid decided against them, writing to Lady Stamford beforehand: 'I rather dread those large pictures in that pretty hall.' They were finally returned in 1979, giving considerable extra balance and colour to the room and proving Macquoid's fears unfounded.

Across the near end of the room copies of Van Dyck's *Charles I* and *Henrietta Maria* confront an 18th-century copy of a portrait of *Thomas, Lord Grey of Groby*, the regicide, below which is a facsimile of Charles I's death-warrant bearing Grey's signature above that of Oliver Cromwell. Between Charles I and his queen hangs a portrait purportedly of *Benjamin Hyde*, an ancestor of the 9th Earl through his mother, Harriet White. Beside the fireplace hangs the *Garter Ribbon*, reputedly given by the King to Hyde to thank him for an unsuccessful attempt to arrange safe passage on one of his ships.

To the right of the entrance door is a portrait of

Lord Grey's father, *Henry Grey, 1st Earl of Stamford*, attributed to Lely's assistant J. B. Gaspars. Opposite, in the doorway, is *Lady Jane Grey*, the Nine Days Queen, and to her right is *William Grey, 9th Earl of Stamford*, for whom the Great Hall was remodelled, by J. Ernest Breun. To the left of the fireplace are mid-18th-century portraits of *the 4th Earl and Countess of Stamford*. Between them is *Maurice, Prince of Orange* in the manner of Michael Miereveldt. Over the fireplace is Jan Looten's late 17th-century *Wooded Landscape with a Village*.

SCULPTURE

A white marble bust of the Emperor Hadrian (head Antique, but neck and shoulders 18th-century), on a pink and grey marble pedestal. Probably acquired by the 5th Earl of Stamford, it has been in the Great Hall since at least 1787. Until 1905 it sat on top of the overmantel.

FURNITURE

Until 1905 the floor of stone and black marble was uncluttered by furniture. Macquoid introduced the present arrangement, which includes some of the finest late 17th- and early 18th-century pieces in the house.

AGAINST WINDOW WALL:

Pair of giltwood side-tables, English, *c.*1730, with Brescia marble tops.

Giltwood pier-glass, English, *c.*1730. The 2nd Earl's monogram beneath an earl's coronet is carved in the cresting.

Eight-day English longcase clock, *c.*1695, by George Graham in a fruitwood case surmounted by gilt brass finials. The case was originally ebonised, but, on Macquoid's advice, it was stripped by Morant & Co. in 1907.

AGAINST FAR WALL:

Oak spice cupboard, English, late 17th-century, the brass key escutcheons engraved with Lord Warrington's monogram and earl's coronet.

Carved walnut hall-bench, English, *c.*1695. The most elaborate of the series of benches acquired by the 6th Earl of Stamford in the early 19th century, the lively carving includes lions on the arms and in the central medallion.

Walnut high-back chairs, English, *c.*1690, four (two against the fireplace wall) of a set of six, almost certainly another acquisition of the 6th Earl of Stamford.

Black and gold lacquer eight-fold screen, Chinese, *c.*1700, with the arms of Richard Savage, 3rd Earl Rivers. Probably acquired by the 9th Earl from Macquoid.

AGAINST FIREPLACE WALL:

Pair of giltwood side-tables, English, *c.*1730, with cream and brown-veined marble tops.

Set of four walnut open armchairs, English, *c.*1670 with pierced dwarf backs and cane seats. Two are in the centre of the room.

An English side-table and pier-glass, c.1730, (Great Hall)

(Opposite) The Great Hall

CENTRE OF ROOM:

Oak refectory table, English, 1908. Made out of two 17th-century tables by Morant & Co., which added the top and the carved frieze, the latter designed by Macquoid. On the table are a *pair of Japanese Imari baluster vases with domed covers and large Imari bowl with shallow domed cover*, early 18th-century; also a *green glass wine bottle* imprinted with the Booth coat of arms, said to have been found in the moat.

Two walnut burgomaster chairs with swivel seats, Flemish, *c.*1730.

METALWORK

Pair of six-light brass chandeliers, late 17th-century. Probably the '2 Brass Chandeliers for 6 Candles each' listed in here in 1758. The large central chandelier and the side-lights were made in 1907 by Rashleigh Phipps & Co. of London, which electrified many of the old light-fittings in the house.

Bronze bell, 17th-century, decorated with a coat of arms, the date 1653, and initials 'BGE' for Sir George Booth (later 1st Lord Delamer) and his second wife, Elizabeth.

Most of the china in the Great Hall is Chinese, Kangxi period (1662–1722), including this massive vase with Buddhist lion finial

CARPET

The large 19th-century Heriz-pattern *Turkey carpet* was bought in 1908.

THE GARDEN ENTRANCE

A continuation of the former screens passage, the garden entrance lies on the central axis of the house and has been the principal way into the garden since the early 18th century. From its half-glazed doors there is a view across the parterre and moat to the North Avenue, which was one of the first to be planted by the 2nd Earl of Warrington. The view terminates in an early 18th-century obelisk just beyond the bank of the Bridgewater Canal, which was cut through the estate in the 1760s.

The wickerwork chairs are Edwardian and were used by the family in the garden. Opposite is a mid-18th-century oak settle, on which the two younger children of Lady Jane Turnbull were required to sit after lunch, when staying at Dunham during the Second World War. To aid their digestion, they had to remain still and quiet for two minutes. The 10th Earl of Stamford, their uncle, would face them from one of the wicker chairs, keeping time with his fob watch. The portrait is of the *4th Earl of Stamford* (incorrectly inscribed 3rd Earl) by Sir Joshua Reynolds, to whom the Earl probably sat in 1756.

Take the door on the right, on entering from the Great Hall.

THE CHAPEL

The Chapel was formed out of two rooms by 'Young' Sir George Booth in 1655, but it was refitted and entirely rebuilt by the 2nd Earl of Warrington in the early 18th century. In keeping with the fierce Protestantism of the family, the decoration is severely restrained, although the quality of workmanship in the oak panelling, pews and reredos is exceptionally high. The blue silk damask above the altar (within the reredos) incorporates the sacred monogram IHS and was woven at Spitalfields in London in the early 18th century. The silk used for the altar frontal and to line the family pew was rewoven by Morant & Co. in 1908–9. The chapel plate, supplied by the

The Chapel

Huguenot goldsmith Isaac Liger in 1706–17, is on display in the Rose Room (see p. 29).

The 1st Lord Delamer's resident chaplain, Adam Martindale, described his duties at Dunham in the 1670s in his autobiography: 'Mine employment there (besides accompanying my Lord oft abroad) was family duty twice a day; which, before dinner, was a short prayer, a chapter and a more solemn prayer; and before supper, the like, only a psalme, or part of one, after the chapter.' He also officiated at 'Lord's-day or King's day' services held in the Chapel and taught Lord Delamer's children mathematics. For all this he was paid £40 per annum, provided his employer was in residence all year, which he often was not, and the sum he actually received was sometimes as little as £12.

The Chapel fell out of use during the late 19th century, and on 20 November 1908 the 9th Earl of Stamford's cousin, Gilbert White, Bishop of Carpentaria in Australia, marked its reopening with a service of Holy Communion. Until the Second World War, the 10th Earl or the Countess led prayers here every morning, a bell over the Kitchen Courtyard being sounded by a housemaid or the butler at five minutes to nine to ensure that every-body was assembled by nine o'clock precisely. The family and any guests would sit in the raised pew at the far end, with the indoor servants below, men on the right and women on the left, all in strict order of precedence. The housekeeper sat in a large wicker-work chair in the centre, immediately below the family.

Cross the Garden Entrance.

THE STONE PARLOUR

This is probably on the site of the Little Parlour of the Tudor house. The family would have eaten here on informal occasions, when only a few of them were at home, and continued to do so well into the 19th century.

In 1906 Compton Hall enlarged the Stone Parlour by taking in the adjoining lamp room, in order to provide a suitable approach to his new Dining Room. He retained the old panelling, which is probably early 18th-century, although in a deliberately old-fashioned style, and added new sections to match, where needed.

PICTURES

The 10th Earl of Stamford acquired all but one of the portraits here, which are either 16th-century or copies of 16th-century originals. They were originally either at Dunham or part of the Enville collection, and include likenesses of Elizabeth Woodville, wife of Sir John de Grey and then of Edward IV, and her daughter, also Elizabeth, who married Henry VII.

FURNITURE

Walnut high-back chairs, English, c.1690, two of a set of six, the others being in the Great Hall.

OPPOSITE WINDOW:

Marquetry side-table and marquetry-framed mirror, both Anglo-Dutch, c.1695.

LEFT OF ENTRANCE DOOR:

Walnut side-table with scagliola top decorated with playing cards, English, c.1715. The game depicted is piquet.

LEFT OF FIREPLACE:

Oak coffer with panelled front, English, c.1670.

LEFT OF WINDOW:

Eight-day striking spring clock in ebonised case by George Graham, London, c.1730.

CERAMICS

Chinese blue-and-white saucer dish, early Kangxi, c.1670–90.

Two Wucai cylindrical vases, one painted with flower and fruit sprays, the other with dragons, Ming/Qing, c.1650.

THE DINING ROOM

The Dining Room can also be viewed from the Kitchen end, later in the tour.

A new dining room in a more convenient location than the old one (which is now the Saloon) was created between 1906 and 1908 out of the former Steward's Room, the adjoining Maids' Room and a back staircase. The conversion was the most ambitious of the internal alterations carried out by Compton Hall for the 9th Earl of Stamford. He removed internal walls, lowered the floor, lengthened the windows, and created a small bay overlooking the moat and parterre. The bay was designed to catch the morning light and to hold a breakfast table, and it was here that most meals were taken when the 10th Earl and Dowager Countess were not entertaining on a large scale, which was generally the case after about 1930. On 17 July 1946, however, when King George VI and Queen Elizabeth came to lunch, the Dining Room was decorated with flowers in much the same way as it would have been for grand lunches and dinners before the First World War: under the direction of the head gardener, Mr Gillies, who had come to Dunham from Sandringham, vases of flowers decorated the table, pots of lilies were grouped in each corner of the room, and the large silver cistern by Philip Rollos was filled with hydrangeas and placed on the side-table opposite the windows.

DECORATION

Compton Hall was responsible for the simple decorative scheme of dark oak and white, which is in considerable contrast to Macquoid's sophisticated use of colour elsewhere. The coat of arms above the fireplace repeats that in the pediment of the south front (see p. 7). The red *brocatelle* curtains are copies of those provided by Morant & Co. in 1908.

PICTURES

In the window bay is a portrait of *Dorothy Wrighte, Countess of Stamford* and the other side of the fireplace is her husband, the *3rd Earl of Stamford* (wrongly inscribed 2nd Earl). Both portraits are attributed to Jonathan Richardson. Opposite the windows, above the side-table, is a portrait of *George Booth of Chester and his Family*. He was a grandson of 'Old' Sir George Booth. On the wall opposite the fireplace, the portrait nearest to the window, by Matthew (?) Ashton, is of *the Hon. Henry Booth*, a younger brother of the 2nd Earl of Warrington.

FURNITURE

Three walnut and gilt side-tables, made in 1821 to support heavy, green-veined marble tops of the 1720s, which form part of the 2nd Earl of Warrington's collection.

The walnut chairs are part of a massive set of 42 distributed throughout the house and clearly added

The Dining Room

to since the first ones were acquired about 1720. The pattern is possibly Chinese-influenced.

The dining-table, the three-tiered *dumb-waiter* and the oval *wine-cooler* are all mahogany, English and late 18th-century.

METALWORK

ON SIDE-TABLE BY STEPS TO STONE PARLOUR:

Brass and copper tea urn or samovar, English, *c.*1770.

Return to the Great Hall and take the doorway in the far left-hand corner. Turn left again to reach the Billiard Room.

THE BILLIARD ROOM

It was common in great houses for there to be at least one principal bedroom at ground-floor level to accommodate an elderly or infirm member of the family. For most of the 18th and 19th centuries, two-thirds of this space were taken up by the Stair Foot Bedroom, the rest being divided into two closets. It was here in 1844 that Katherine, Lady Grey of Groby, the widowed daughter-in-law of the 6th Earl of Stamford, died at the age of 43. She was subsequently laid out in the room, and her niece, Maria Walsh (known as Minny), witnessed the scene at the age of eight. She later recalled being particularly struck by the white kid gloves which were put on Lady Grey's hands.

Compton Hall created a billiard room here in place of that in the Queen Anne Room on the first floor. In order to allow sufficient playing room around the table, the fireplace had to be reconstructed at the far end of the room, which Compton Hall regretted. By the 1930s billiards were rarely being played at Dunham. A housemaid employed at the time remembers her meticulous daily cleaning of the room as seeming somewhat pointless.

DECORATION

The panelling is of an early 18th-century pattern, but may have been introduced by Compton Hall, who was also responsible for the plain white decoration, about which Macquoid wrote disparagingly in 1907: 'I think you will find eventually that you will not like a white-billiard room but the colour is a good one to produce a clean bright effect over with another colour, should you like to change it some day.'

SCULPTURE

At the far end of the room are three wax busts by Richard Cockle Lucas (1800–83), dated 1832, of *the 6th Earl of Stamford* and his grandchildren, *George Harry* and *Margaret Grey*.

FURNITURE

The billiard-table by Burroughes and Watts is mid-19th-century. The *marker board* and *mace-headed cues* were provided by Gillows and are associated with an earlier table. Other items came from Thurstons.

METALWORK

The brass six-light billiard pendant was provided by Farraday & Son of London in 1908.

TEXTILES

The tapestry curtains of c.1908 were probably woven by L. H. Lee Ltd of Warrington and Liverpool.

The printed cotton cover, intended to protect the billiard-table from dust, dates from about 1920 and is an unusual survival.

THE GRAND STAIRCASE

This staircase is on the site of that constructed by Sir George Booth, 1st Bt, in about 1600. The 2nd Earl of Warrington's decision to replace it in solid mahogany, when he rebuilt the house in the 1730s, was not as extravagant as it might seem: mahogany was at times cheaper than good oak in the early 18th century. It was also a practical choice, being imported in large planks suitable for structural as well as decorative use.

When Dunham Massey was being used as a hospital during the First World War, the staircase also served as an operating theatre, as it was close to the principal ward in the Saloon and had running water available in an adjoining lavatory. It was not, however, well lit and Lady Jane Turnbull, who assisted at operations as a nurse, had to hold a torch on one occasion to allow the surgeon to see to remove a bullet lodged in a soldier's brain.

DECORATION

The delicate ceiling plasterwork was added in 1778 by George Cockram, who embellished the Great Gallery ceiling a few years later. The yellow wall colour was probably chosen by Macquoid.

PICTURES

To either side of the door from the Great Hall is a pair of mid-17th-century portraits of *Sir John Langham, 1st Bt*, and his wife *Mary Bunce*, the grandparents of *Mary Langham, Countess of Warrington* whose portrait by Jonathan Richardson hangs to the right of the Billiard Room door. Above the first flight of stairs is a full-length, after Van Dyck, of *Henry Danvers, 1st Earl of Danby*, a distinguished soldier and Royalist. To his left is *Colonel Sir John Booth*, fifth son of Sir George Booth, 1st Bt, painted about 1640. Colonel Booth was imprisoned in the Tower in 1651 for complicity in a plot to restore Charles II, by whom he was later knighted.

At the head of the next flight is a portrait by George Sandars of *George Harry, 7th Earl of Stamford, and his sister Margaret, as children*, painted in 1833.

SCULPTURE

The early 19th-century busts within the window reveals are of *Lord* and *Lady Grey of Groby*, the parents of the 7th Earl.

CARPET

The stair carpet was rewoven in Kidderminster in 1996. The original was probably supplied in 1855, when the east-range rooms were being refitted for the 7th Earl's second Countess, Catherine Cocks. It was of various colours, but was overdyed red between 1905 and 1910.

Ascend the short flight of stairs from the upper landing.

THE GREEN SILK ROOM

In 1758 this was the Brown Silk Damask Bedchamber, its bed, windows and walls hung with a rare and costly Chinese silk, some of which survives in store. From the late 18th century until 1905, the room was one of a suite occupied by successive Countesses of Stamford. It was comprehensively refurnished in the mid-1850s for the 7th Earl's second Countess, the former bare-back rider Catherine Cocks, becoming her boudoir and being filled with typically exuberant mid-Victorian furniture in stark contrast to the sobriety of 18th- and early 19th-century Dunham.

Catherine Cocks, Countess of Stamford

The Green Silk Room

The green-ground chenille carpet, chandelier by Osler of Birmingham, gilt pelmets, huge pier-glass and associated table, pair of papier-mâché chairs with historical scenes by Jennens and Bettridge and the Louis XV-style tables were all part of the scheme and can be seen in late 19th-century photographs.

The Countess only ever occupied the room for a few days in 1856, Dunham being abandoned as a residence thereafter because of the hostility of local people to her lowly origins. The decorative and furnishing schemes, however, survived untouched into the 20th century and were merely toned down as part of the Edwardian restoration of the house for the 9th Earl and Countess. Because of the location of what was now called the Green Silk Room at the head of the Grand Stairs, and its sweeping views over the garden, it was chosen as the bedroom for the exiled Emperor Haile Selassie of Ethiopia during his stay at Dunham in 1938. The Equestrienne Countess's coroneted bed was introduced from the adjoining room (not open) and palms were hoisted on to the flat roof outside whilst the Summer Parlour, on the other side of the Grand Staircase, was turned over to his sitting room.

PICTURES

Over the fireplace is a chalk portrait of *Mrs Ward*, granddaughter of the 5th Earl of Stamford, by John Hayter. To either side are engravings of the *7th Earl and Countess* above late 19th-century watercolour views of Corsica by John Cowen. Above the bed is an engraving of Landseer's *Windsor Castle in the present time*. The picture to its left is executed in hair. Opposite are two watercolour coastal scenes by Anthony Vandyke Copley between which is an engraving of *the 7th Earl and his sister, Lady Mary Milbank, as children*. Their parents, *Lord and Lady Grey of Groby*, are depicted in the miniatures by Sir Charles Ross on the desk below.

THE SUMMER PARLOUR

Originally known as the Velvet Bedchamber, this was one of two state bedrooms at either end of the Great Gallery and, like the Billiard Room below, it was divided into three rooms with two closets at the far end. Compton Hall removed the partitions and inserted the present fireplace in the early 20th

century to create an antiquarian bedroom, called the King Charles Room.

Lady Stamford probably abandoned the idea of the King Charles Room in favour of the Summer Parlour during the First World War, when the other sitting rooms were occupied by the hospital. The room became a great favourite with both Lady Stamford and the 10th Earl, having fine views over the garden and catching the evening sun. Lord Stamford continued to make use of it for sitting and talking with family and friends, sometimes also taking tea here, until the end of his life.

DECORATION

As in the Billiard Room below, the panelling is possibly early 18th-century, rearranged and added to by Compton Hall, who once again applied two coats of white paint to the woodwork.

PICTURES

The picture hang was largely set before the room became the Summer Parlour and thus mainly relates to Charles I and the Stuart court. Either side of the entrance door are copies of two well-known Van Dycks, *Sir Endymion Porter and his family* and *Thomas Wentworth, Earl of Strafford and Sir Philip Mainwaring*. To the right of the door of the Great Gallery is a portrait of Charles I's daughter, *Henrietta Anne Stuart, Duchess of Orleans*, after Henri and Charles Beaubrun.

The room is dominated by a later introduction, the full-length by J. Ernest Breun of *Penelope Theobald, Countess of Stamford, and her two children*. Lady Jane Grey (later Turnbull) is depicted clasping Breun's studio cat. The portrait on the easel is also of *Lady Jane Turnbull*, by Margaret Lindsay Williams, painted at the request of Lady Stamford for her 90th birthday. Lady Jane was 56 at the time, but, in accordance with her mother's specific instructions, grey hairs and wrinkles were not shown.

PHOTOGRAPHS

On the table at the near end of the room are photographs of the 10th Earl and his sister as children and of Canon Theobald (Lady Stamford's father). There is also a group photograph of the Emperor and Crown Prince of Ethiopia with the 10th Earl and his mother in the garden at Dunham on 12 June 1938.

FURNITURE

Much of the furniture here is late 18th-century or Regency, including the *bergère chairs* in Edwardian floral upholstery, *the sofa, the rosewood sofa-table* of *c.*1820, *the mahogany bureau* of *c.*1780, and the set of *ebonised and rush-seated chairs*, their backs painted with flowers, also *c.*1820.

Other pieces of interest include *the walnut and gilt side-table* of *c.*1720 at the far end of the room, which is *en suite* with those in the Dining Room, and a pair of contemporary *plain walnut close-stools* of the same date on either side of the fireplace. The *walnut fire-screen* incorporating stuffed humming birds and butterflies on flowered branches was made for the 7th Earl and Countess of Stamford, *c.*1860, for their house at Bradgate in Leicestershire, and was bought from there by the 10th Earl in 1925. The *painted chairs and stool* upholstered in blue velvet in front of the bookcase by the entrance door are from the coronation of George VI in 1937 which both the 10th Earl and the Dowager Countess attended. On the early 18th-century oak *gate-leg table* at the near end of the room is a late 18th-century *Chinese export black lacquer casket* given in 1849 as a wedding present to Harriet Grey, mother of the 9th Earl of Stamford. *The eight-day English striking spring clock* on the mantelshelf is by George Graham of London, *c.*1700. *The eight-day French striking spring clock* in a Boulle case on a side-table at the far end is by Gaudon, Paris, *c.*1720.

CERAMICS

The bottles and jugs are mainly Japanese, Imari, early 18th-century.

THE GREAT GALLERY

Like so many other rooms of the 2nd Earl of Warrington's house, the Great Gallery is almost certainly the reconstruction of a pre-existing space. A 'Long Gallery' is recorded in the inventory undertaken after the death of the 1st Earl in 1694, and it was probably in here that Katherine Booth, Lord Warrington's second cousin, was instructed to sit at the feet of the Duke of Monmouth during his visit to Dunham in September 1682. According to her own account, she had to 'tell him who everybody was and many things he asked me, and when he danced he made me dance with him (tho' I had never learnt)'.

Allegory with Venus, Mars, Cupid and Time; *by Guercino (Great Gallery)*

In 1783–4 the room was refurbished for the 2nd Earl's grandson, the 5th Earl of Stamford. The ceiling was decorated by George Cockram with plaster rosettes designed by John Hope, a new chimneypiece by Samuel Hope was introduced, and the sash-windows were changed. The chimneypiece was replaced with the present one in the early 19th century, at the same time as the splendid Regency grate and fender were introduced.

By the mid-19th century the room had become heavily furnished and was known as the Drawing Room. It was perhaps the only space in the house to have been redecorated during the tenancy of Robert Platt (1869–82). In the early 20th century only minor repairs to the plasterwork were needed but the death of the 9th Earl in 1910 brought work to a halt, and the Gallery was thereafter used to store some of the surplus contents of the house. Over 250 pieces of furniture, together with rolled carpets, cushions, metalwork and other objects, were arranged in neat rows, cleaned daily until the Second World War. An area was kept clear at the Summer Parlour end of the room to accommodate a billiard-table, upon which the 10th Earl and his sister could play billiard fives with their guests. Lady Stamford would not allow this somewhat boisterous game in the Billiard Room.

DECORATION

The Great Gallery remained a store in 1976 on the death of the 10th Earl, and when it was redecorated in 1979, the joinery scheme introduced by the Platts was followed, with the walls being painted in a

(Above) The Great Gallery, showing three of the famous bird's-eye views

pinkish-red similar to a colour employed elsewhere by Macquoid. Two new Savonnerie-style carpets were woven for either end of the room in 1981, and festoon curtains were made for the windows.

PICTURES

The views of Dunham displayed here form one of the most remarkable and comprehensive surveys of a country house ever painted. To the left of the fireplace, above the side-table, is the earliest, *Dunham Massey from the South-east* by Adriaen van Diest, which was painted in 1697 and shows the Jacobean house with its mid-17th-century south range and forecourt and the first of the many avenues planted by the 2nd Earl of Warrington.

The four other views, *Dunham Massey from the South, South-east, South-west* and *North*, were painted by John Harris in 1751, probably to commemorate the transformation of the house and park over the previous half-century by Lord Warrington. They are a unique record of an 18th-century formal landscape, taken just as such layouts were being rendered old-fashioned by the naturalistic approach of 'Capability' Brown, and they are also amongst the last paintings of country houses ever to be produced in the form of the 'bird's-eye view'. Two more straightforward landscapes by Harris, survivors of a set of three *Views of the Peak* recorded in 1769, hang on the fireplace wall, to the left of the exit door. Over the fireplace is a 17th-century copy of Sebastiano del Piombo's *Ferry Candolet and his Secretary*, which was probably acquired by the 2nd Earl.

At the far end of the room is the finest picture in the house, Guercino's oval *Allegory with Venus, Mars, Cupid and Time*, painted towards the beginning of his career, around 1624–6, and anticipating a later treatment of the same rare subject painted for the Count of Württemberg in 1656. The theme is love and its dangerous consequences, with Cupid being trapped under a net by Venus, who was later to be similarly treated following a dalliance with Mars – hence the warning presence of Time. The picture is in its original frame and the eight-point stars with which it is decorated must relate to the original patron, but as yet he remains unidentified. The Dunham Guercino is thought to have been acquired by the 4th Earl of Stamford at the sale of the collection of John Blackwood in 1754.

To the left of the Guercino is a near-contemporary three-quarter-length copy of the Holbein full-length of *Christina, Duchess of Milan*. She was one of Henry VIII's prospective brides after the death of Jane Seymour. Above is *Henry Grey, 1st Earl of Stamford* by Cornelius Johnson. Over the doors are portraits of *'Old' Sir George Booth, 1st Bt*, the *Countesses of Berkshire* and *Oxford and Elgin*, sisters-in-law of the 1st Earl of Stamford, and a 17th-century copy after Guido Reni of *Aurora*. Between the windows are Pietro Antoniani's *An Eruption of Vesuvius* and an 18th-century Venetian artist's view of *The Entrance to the Canareggio, Venice*.

SCULPTURE

The 17th-century marble statuettes of Dacian Kings on scagliola pedestals flanking the fireplace imitate the classical taste for coloured marbles as well as for statues of captive barbarians. Dacia (in modern Romania) was conquered by the Roman Emperor Trajan in AD 105.

FURNITURE

The four carved benches, of the 1690s, were probably acquired by the 6th Earl of Stamford in the early 19th century. The pair with carved lions on their canted arms were at that time adapted to stand in the window bays of the Great Hall, but were displaced by radiators in the early 20th century. The handsome *pair of mahogany side-tables* with white marble tops, *c*.1730, was also acquired for the Great Hall, where it remained until 1905. The large set of *sabre-legged mahogany chairs* was acquired for the room *c*.1830 and is probably from Gillows of Lancaster. They currently lack their seat pads. *The*

mahogany breakfast-table in the centre of the room is of about 1800. *One of four walnut and gilt side-tables* with early 18th-century marble tops, introduced to the room by the 6th Earl, has recently been returned and stands near the door to the Queen Anne Room.

MUSICAL INSTRUMENTS

The square piano by Broadwood was bought for £68 5s in 1840. The *boudoir grand piano* in a rosewood case at the other end of the room was made by Bechstein in 1894, and was previously in the Great Hall. It was on this instrument during the Second World War that a visiting Russian diplomat played the Red Flag. Lord Stamford was able to sing along, as he had been taught the words by the wife of Ramsay MacDonald's Chancellor of the Exchequer, Philip Snowden.

CERAMICS

The finest examples of Japanese porcelain in the house are on display here: *nine early 18th-century Imari baluster vases* on the mahogany side-tables and, over the fireplace, *three hexagonal Kakiemon vases* with shallow domed covers, *c*.1690, decorated in the distinctive palette typical of Kakiemon ware. None of these is recorded in the house before the 19th century, and they may have been acquired by the 6th Earl in the early 19th century.

Against the window wall is *a pair of massive faience jardinières*, possibly Spanish, mid-18th-century.

THE QUEEN ANNE ROOM

Originally the Yellow Damask Bedchamber, or Great Bedchamber, this was the most important of the two state bedrooms in the 18th century. In 1758 it was richly furnished, with 'Yellow Genoa Damask' covering the state bed, a settee, ten chairs and two stools, as well as being used for the window curtains. It was for this room that the 2nd Earl of Warrington bought the magnificent set of silver sconces, or wall-lights, four of which can be seen in the Rose Room.

In 1830 a billiard-table was installed here and the room continued to be used for billiards until reverting to being a bedroom in the early 20th century. It was then dubbed the Queen Anne Room for no other apparent reason than its early 18th-century date. During the First World War

Lady Stamford adopted the room as her bedroom, which it remained until her death in 1959. It is now used to display Dunham's late 17th-century state bed and Lady Mary Booth, Countess of Stamford's silver toilet service. The room was redecorated in 2005 with a crimson flock wallpaper of an Edwardian pattern known as 'Genoese'.

PICTURES

Over the fireplace is a portrait of *Mary Langham, Countess of Warrington* (wife of the 1st Earl) by Jacob Huysmans. Opposite is Michael Dahl's *2nd Earl of Warrington and his daughter Lady Mary Booth*, the latter holding a sheet of music by Purcell.

FURNITURE

Dunham Massey's state bed survives in a remarkably complete state and has recently been conserved after nearly a century in store. It dates from the early 1680s and passed to the 2nd Earl of War-

rington from his great-aunt, Sarah Alston, Duchess of Somerset. In the 18th and 19th centuries it was treated as an heirloom and displayed in the Velvet Bedchamber (now the Summer Parlour). It was sent away to Morant & Co. for restoration by the 9th Earl of Stamford, but after his death in 1910 it came back untouched and remained in its packing cases until being rediscovered by the National Trust in the 1970s. Also displayed are a *set of five walnut stools*, English, *c.*1690, with carved and pierced stretchers, covered in 18th-century red floral damask and a *set of six high-backed walnut chairs*, *c.*1695, in the style of the Huguenot designer Daniel Marot. *The burr-walnut close-stool of c.*1710, which originally housed a silver chamber-pot and is edged with ebony and inlaid with Lord Warrington's monogram, was recorded in one of the closets to this room in 1758 together with the matching *burr-walnut chest*.

SILVER

In the showcase between the windows is a full toilet service, made in 1754, mostly by Magdalen Feline and probably a 50th birthday present for the 2nd Earl of Warrington's daughter, Lady Mary Booth, Countess of Stamford. The dressing-table on which the service is set is covered in crimson silk, as was the case in the Countess's bed chamber (The Bishop's Room) in 1758. The white linen cloth was used to protect the silk, and the backcloth was for covering the service when not in use. It is from this cloth, or toilette, that such services gain their name.

THE QUEEN ANNE STAIRS

To the right of the staircase is a portrait of the 2nd Earl of Warrington's daughter, *Lady Mary Booth as a Child*, by Michael Dahl. *A Dutch Mastiff*, hanging on the opposite wall, is probably by Jan Wyck. It is thought to be of 'Pugg, alias Old Vertue', whose gravestone dated 1702 can still be seen in the North Avenue beyond the moat. Behind the door from the Great Gallery is a mahogany fuse box and a framed list of circuits dating from the introduction of electricity in 1906.

(Left) The State Bed in the Queen Anne Room

THE TEA ROOM

Tea would have been served here in the 18th century, usually after dinner and with some ritual, as leaf tea was then a highly priced luxury. Coffee and chocolate would also have been drunk, and in 1758, on the death of Lord Warrington, a 'Silver Chocolate Pott' and '2 Silver Coffee Potts on 2 Waiters' were in the room in addition to all the tea silver. The 10th Earl of Stamford sometimes took breakfast in the Tea Room. His bedroom (not currently on show) was next door, and a concealed staircase leads up from the Kitchen.

PICTURES

As young men, both the 5th and 6th Earls of Stamford travelled to Italy on the Grand Tour, and some of their purchases are shown here. Two large caricatures painted by Thomas Patch in 1760 depict the 5th Earl of Stamford, with his prominent chin accentuated, in company with his friends. In one, he is engaged in the serious study of monuments at Pula on the Croatian coast; in the other, he is enjoying an evening at Mr Hatfield's Inn in Florence. In the latter the artist has introduced a caricature bust of himself on the right-hand wall. The 5th Earl is also depicted in the portrait by Anton Raphael Mengs over the fireplace, and, with his travelling companion, Sir Henry Mainwaring, 4th Bt, in a painting by Nathaniel Dance on the window wall which was returned to Dunham in 2005 with the assistance of the V & A Purchase Grant Fund, the Art Fund and the Whiteley family. In the display case beneath is a miniature version of the same subject, shown alongside Grand Tour diaries and guides.

Opposite the fireplace are three large watercolours of views near Rome, two of *The Temple of Minerva Medica* and one of *The Cascade at Terni*. These were painted in 1788 by the Swiss artist Louis Ducros for the 6th Earl.

To the left of the fireplace is a pair of oval portraits of *the 4th Earl* and *Countess of Stamford*.

SCULPTURE

On the side-table opposite the fireplace are 18th-century Italian-school marble models of the columns of the Temples of Castor and Pollux and of Vespasian in the Roman Forum.

FURNITURE

The furniture includes a *mahogany Shovette board* by F. H. Ayre of London, *c.*1910. The object of this game, usually pronounced 'shove it', was to get the counters as near as possible to, or in, the central pit. It was played at Dunham Massey during the house parties of the 1920s.

THE ROSE GALLERY

Named after the rooms off it, the Rose Gallery contains some early 18th-century mahogany chests and a series of watercolour views in and around the park at Dunham Massey painted by Anthony Devis in 1767. These include depictions of the New Park, which was laid out by the Countess of Stamford in the 1760s, possibly to the design of 'Capability' Brown. The leather-upholstered chair at the near end is of the mid-18th century, whilst the chair at the far end is from the coronation of George V in 1911, which the Countess attended alone, the 9th Earl having died the previous year.

THE ROSE ROOM

In the mid-18th century this was the Crimson Damask Dressing Room and was one of the suite of rooms occupied by Lady Mary Booth, Countess of Stamford. It was refitted in the early 19th century when the mahogany window cornices (probably by Gillows) were introduced and 18th-century Chinese brown silk damask curtains were brought from elsewhere in the house. They were rewoven in 2004 to a pattern similar to those originally in the room. The red ingrain paper is Edwardian. In the 20th century the room was used by Lady Jane Turnbull, the 10th Earl's sister, when visiting Dunham after her marriage.

PICTURE

The portrait of *George Booth, 2nd Earl of Warrington* (1675–1758), is by an unknown English artist, *c.*1720.

SILVER

During his 64-year tenure of Dunham Massey, the 2nd Earl of Warrington accumulated over 1,000 pieces of silver, weighing 26,000 ounces – all of the exceptional quality expected of the Huguenot silversmiths whom he patronised, and all meticulously recorded in his own hand in an inventory entitled *The Particular of My Plate*. What survives here today is about one-sixth of the original, but still a prodigious quantity representing one of the largest groups of plate made for a single patron to remain in the house for which it was commissioned.

In the mid-19th century the entire collection was removed to Enville Hall in Staffordshire, which passed to a different branch of the family on the death of the 7th Earl of Stamford's widow in 1905. It was only with the two Enville sales of 1921 and 1931 that the 10th Earl of Stamford was able to buy back much of what can now be seen, and his policy of reacquisition has been followed by the National Trust. Recent purchases have been made possible with the assistance of the A. H. & B. C. Whiteley Trust, the Heritage Lottery Fund, the Art Fund, the V&A Purchase Grant Fund and the Monument Trust. The National Trust is also indebted to the Manchester City Art Gallery, the Goldsmiths' Company and Lord Deramore for the loan of other items.

BUFFET CASE:

On an early 18th-century mahogany side-table covered in white linen is the display plate, traditionally placed on a tiered buffet or sideboard to impress visitors with the wealth and status of the host. Much of it is associated with the service of wine including the *water fountain* (Peter Archambo c.1728) and the *cistern* in the centre (Philip Rollos, 1701), their handles in the form of boars alluding to Lord Warrington's coat of arms. They were used for washing wine glasses between courses. The two *tankards* were made by Thomas Jenkins in 1671 and are engraved with the arms of Sir James Langham, 2nd Bt, the father-in-law of the 1st Earl of Warrington. These tankards were particularly revered by subsequent generations, and Lady Mary Booth, Countess of Stamford, stipulated in her Will that they should always remain at Dunham. The triangular *egg-cup frame with ten egg-cups* (Peter Archambo, 1741) is the earliest known example in silver surviving in Europe and probably even in the world. Boiled or coddled eggs were particularly popular in the early 18th century.

TO THE RIGHT OF BUFFET CASE:

The large *cistern* (Peter Archambo, 1729) was intended for wine bottles which would have been packed with ice to keep them cool. In the 18th

century both red and white wine were drunk cold. The mahogany stand is contemporary.

IN CASE BETWEEN WINDOWS:

The chapel plate survives intact and is all by Isaac Liger. The *alms-dish* (superbly engraved by Simon Gribelin with a *Deposition* after Annibale Carracci), the *chalice, paten* and *flagon* are all of 1706, the tripod *altar candlesticks* being added ten years later, and a small '*offering bason*' or alms-dish in 1717.

IN CASE OPPOSITE BUFFET PLATE, FROM LEFT:

Silver for lighting is well represented at Dunham Massey. The finest surviving items are the *four sconces* or wall-lights (Peter Archambo, 1730), each of which has a different mythological scene depicted on its back. Many of the plain candlesticks, for general use about the house, were made by Isaac Liger. Each pair would have had snuffers and a snuffer tray but only one of the latter (by Paul de Lamerie, 1729) is at Dunham today. The *four candelabra* are later, being commissioned from Parker & Wakelin by Lord Warrington's grandson, the 5th Earl of Stamford, in 1773–4.

Amongst the chamber plate, for washing and use about the house, are two circular *wash ball boxes* which were intended for soap. Lord Warrington's own *hand bell* (Peter Archambo, 1738) is on display here with a *standish* (inkstand) of 1716 and a smaller *bell* of 1729, both by Isaac Liger. The *chamberpot* (Daniel Piers, 1747) is one of the fifteen originally commissioned for Dunham.

There are *waiters* or *salvers* for a variety of purposes including 'to give drink on', 'to give tea on' and for the teapots. A large number is associated with the service of dessert, including six 'not gilt' by Peter Archambo, 1732, beautifully engraved with Lord Warrington's monogram, and three gilt by David Willaume, 1743.

Silver which would have been on the dining-table during a meal includes *plates, salt cellars* and silver-gilt *finger-bowls*, all by Peter Archambo, and two impressive *tureens* by David Willaume, 1740.

IN CASE OPPOSITE WINDOWS:

The two huge *salvers* (or tables as they were known in the 18th century) on mahogany stands were intended for serving coffee (the smaller of the two, by James Schruder, 1741) and tea (David Willaume the Younger, 1741). The tea kettle and lamp are by Edward Feline, 1746.

THE STAMFORD GALLERY

The Countess probably chose the striped paper, which was supplied by Morant & Co., together with the green damask curtains, in 1909.

PICTURES

The engravings, paintings and drawings are predominantly 18th-century, and include Grand Tour views and a series of landscapes painted around 1790 by Lady Maria Cotes and Lady Louisa Grey, daughters of the 5th Earl of Stamford.

FURNITURE

The magnificent collection of early 18th-century *walnut chests* was probably gathered together here after the First World War by the 10th Earl. Some of the chests were intended for keeping documents and plans and are recorded in Lord Warrington's business room (now the Oak Bedroom) in 1758, whilst others stood in bedrooms. Their form and the quality of their veneers and ebony inlays suggest they were made by a leading London cabinetmaker, as yet unidentified, who was working about 1710. The *mahogany chest* with a domed lid at the near end could be the 'large Mahogany Chest, Drawers I[n] th[e] Bottom' which was here on its own amongst tables and bookcases in 1758.

THE BLUE CHINTZ BEDROOM

This room lies behind the pedimented centrepiece of the house and was known in the 18th century as the Centre Bedchamber. The cornice, chests-of-drawers fitted neatly into the window recesses, and the fireplace were introduced in 1789, when all the rooms off the Stamford Gallery were refitted for the 5th Earl of Stamford following the alteration of the south front. The iron grate is probably one of those 'with as little ornament on them as possible' requested by Lady Stamford from the architect John Hope in January 1789.

In the early 19th century the room was adopted by the 6th Earl as his bedroom, and the green-lined chintz hangings from that time were retained by Penelope, Countess of Stamford, when she redecorated following the return of the family in 1905. The furniture is predominantly late Georgian and Regency and much of it was probably supplied by Gillows of Lancaster. The pictures include engravings of *Sir John Walsh, 1st Bt* (later 1st Baron Ormathwaite) and of his wife, *Lady Jane Grey, with their daughter Maria Katherine* (known as Minny).

THE BLUE CHINTZ DRESSING ROOM

An earlier Lady Jane Grey, Queen for nine days in July 1553, is celebrated here in a collection of 18th- and 19th-century prints giving romanticised depictions of episodes in her brief and tragic life. There are also two watercolours of the ruins of Bradgate House in Leicestershire, which was Lady Jane's childhood home and, until being abandoned in the early 18th century, the principal seat of the Earls of Stamford.

THE ST THOMAS BEDROOM

In the early 19th century this was the bedroom of the 6th Earl's eldest son, George Harry, Lord Grey of Groby. He suffered from severe mental fits and was subjected to the horrifying treatments then considered appropriate. In 1833, according to Sir John Walsh, he was bled by one doctor and afterwards seen by another who:

… declared that there was not a minute to lose, that paralysis, and apoplexy were staring them in the face, and he immediately repeated the bleeding freely, upon which Grey recovered his consciousness for a minute or two, and asked where he was. Leeches were afterwards applied to his head and she [Lady Grey] says that it was the most dreadful sight to witness his delirium whilst they were on. His screams, and endeavours to pluck them off, and his exclaiming constantly, I am dying, I tell you I am dying.

Lord Grey recovered on this occasion, but died two years later, aged 33.

The early 19th-century printed cotton bed-hangings were probably brought here from elsewhere in the house by Lady Stamford, who chose the wallpaper, and, in 1907, embroidered the bedspread. By the door is an engraving of Lord Grey's children, George Harry (later 7th Earl) and Lady Margaret, with a caged parrot. Parrots were kept at Dunham well into the 20th century. Beneath is the stool depicted in the engraving.

THE STAMFORD BATHROOM

At the near end of the Stamford Gallery is one of the six bathrooms introduced to Dunham by Compton Hall for the 9th Earl. Its tessellated floor, Dutch-tile wallpaper treated with a wipeable (now yellowed) varnish, and its splendid fittings are all Edwardian and represent the best that was available at the time. The luxurious crocodile-skin suitcase fitted with pouches, pockets and boxes for all manner of toilet-ware was made by Finnigans of Manchester and was given to the 10th Earl on his coming-of-age in 1917. The semicircular mahogany commode is late 18th-century.

Adjacent to the bathroom is a housemaids' sluice, also intact, which allowed waste and water from the Stamford Gallery bedrooms to be disposed of without having to be carried through the house. The lavatory serving the bedrooms can be seen at the far end of the gallery.

THE OAK BEDROOM

This was originally the 2nd Earl of Warrington's reading or business room – hence the inset book-shelves to either side of the fireplace. On the Earl's death in 1758 the room contained mahogany tables, a writing-desk, chests and cabinets for documents and leases and the '2 large Looking Glasses

fixt in the Wainscot' which are still in place. Penelope, Countess of Stamford, perhaps advised by Macquoid, brought in the 1830s bed and the printed cotton hangings, which were produced in Lancashire about 1810. This is one of the earliest of the printed cottons in Dunham's extensive collection and is particularly effective here against the hand-blocked, originally brightly coloured, wallpaper of about the same date. The wallpaper fills the spaces hung with painted striped cloth in the 18th century.

To the right of the fireplace is an example of the telephones introduced by Compton Hall throughout the house as part of a sophisticated internal communication system. There would originally have been another telephone to the left of the fireplace: one was connected to the Butler's Pantry, should food be required, and the other was to summon a maid for hot water or to attend to the fire. Above the bell pushes associated with the telephones are discreet labels incised with the destination of the line and the instruction 'RING TWICE TO SPEAK'.

PICTURE

RIGHT OF ENTRANCE DOOR:

HUGH DOUGLAS HAMILTON (1734–1808)
The Hon. George Grey and Miss Henrietta Grey as Children with their Nurse
The eldest children of the 5th Earl. George Grey succeeded his father as 6th Earl in 1819. Henrietta married Sir John Chetwode, 4th Bt.

THE LIBRARY

The Library is one of the least changed of the early 18th-century interiors, and its fitted oak bookcases contain many of the volumes collected by its creator, the 2nd Earl of Warrington. His books are identified by the monogram and earl's coronet stamped on their spines, and reflect his interest in religion, politics, genealogy and history. Science is also covered, and Lord Warrington was responsible for acquiring the three astronomical instruments in the room, all of which are by Thomas Wright,

(Left) The cotton fabric in the Oak Bedroom was printed in Lancashire about 1810 and is among the earliest examples in the collection

instrument-maker to George II. The largest and most complex of these, known as an orrery after the 4th Earl of Orrery, for whom one of the first was made, is of about 1730. It has a mechanism which allows the movements of the planets around the sun to be demonstrated in relation to each other and to their own satellites. The orrery has its original oak stand and cover, as does the slightly earlier armillary sphere, which shows the relationship of the meridian, equator and other celestial rings to the planets. The telescope is probably contemporary with the orrery and is of the reflecting type first constructed by Sir Isaac Newton in 1668, but not commonly available until the 1730s.

STAINED GLASS

To preserve the fragile contents of the Library, the blinds have to be drawn over the stained glass. On request, the blind at the near end can be temporarily lifted to allow viewing.

The upper parts of the three windows contain a collection of exceptionally fine 17th-century stained glass, which is predominantly Flemish. In the first window are three of an incomplete set of the *Labours of the Months* together with the twelve *Sibyls*, the latter accompanied by inscriptions. Other panels include three architectural views, probably early 17th-century, and some highly dramatic biblical scenes, including an *Annunciation* and two *Seasons* executed in monochrome to a very high standard and surviving in remarkably good condition. The glass is known to have been repaired in 1833 and again, by Morant & Co., in

1911. Further work was undertaken in 1996 with the help of the East Cheshire Association of the National Trust.

CARVING

The carving of the *Crucifixion* over the fireplace is the earliest known work by Grinling Gibbons. He was working on it when he was discovered by John Evelyn in 1671. Evelyn recorded in his diary for 18 January that year:

I this day first acquainted his Majestie [Charles II] with that incomparable young man, Gibson [*sic*] whom I lately found in … a poore solitary thatched house in a field in our Parish [Deptford] … carving that large Cartoone or Crucifix of Tintorets, a Copy of which I had also myselfe brought from Venice….

The relief is based upon Agostino Carracci's engraving of Tintoretto's painting in the Scuola di San Rocco, Venice, and follows the details so precisely that Evelyn was prompted to remark that he had never before seen such 'studious exactness'. Evelyn's introduction assured Gibbons of royal patronage, but it was actually Sir George Viner who 'not long after' acquired the piece, for £80. The carving had probably entered Lord Warrington's collection by the time the Library was constructed, and is first recorded at Dunham in 1758.

FURNITURE

The *mahogany centre-table* and *walnut chest* on a later mahogany stand are of about 1720. The *walnut splat-back chairs* with heavy cabriole legs are slightly earlier. The *oak library steps* were bought in 1838, while the pair of *leather-upholstered arm-chairs* are of *c.*1760.

THE GREY STAIRS

Named after Lord Grey, whose rooms it served in the early 19th century, this staircase leads up to the nursery floor (not open to the public). On the landing is a 19th-century hand-operated fire trolley and an 18th-century painting of *A Mastiff with a Small Dog* which includes a depiction of the *mahogany table trolley and beer cask,* placed below it. The trolley, which is a rare survival, was intended for the servants' hall table and allowed servants to help themselves to beer, the staple drink of most households until the mid-19th century. Opposite the window is the hatchment which was hung on the front of the house in 1854 after the death of the 7th Earl's first countess, Elizabeth (known as Bessie) Billage. She did not have her own coat of arms, and so her side of the hatchment, which is to the right and has a black background to indicate that she had

The Crucifixion; *by the great 17th-century wood-carver Grinling Gibbons (Library)*

died, is filled with artistic swirls. At the bottom of the stairs are paintings by Daniel Clowes of dogs which belonged to the 5th Earl, and opposite them is the 10th Earl's bicycle, which he always kept here. Over the Study door are some of the bells by which footmen were summoned from the late 18th century until the advent of the electric bell and telephone system in the early 1900s.

THE STUDY

This was the Common Parlour of Lord Warrington's house, where he and his family would generally have eaten when entertaining informally rather than in state. Under the Edwardian reorganisation it and the two following rooms were allocated to Lord Stamford as his study, secretary's room and receiving room.

The 10th Earl used the Study constantly, and his life is reflected in its contents. There are portraits of his mother and father (by Edward Clifford and F. S. Ogilvy respectively), and photographs of statesmen and world leaders he knew through his involvement in the League of Nations. Lord Stamford was a great admirer of the American president Woodrow Wilson and a loyal friend of Haile Selassie, Emperor of Ethiopia, whose very public visit to Dunham Massey in 1938, after being ousted by the Italians, was contrary to British policy. It marked the start of a long association between the two men, which was ended only by the Emperor's murder in 1975, a year after having once again been dethroned. Photographs, pamphlets and press cuttings relating to Haile Selassie are on show in the display case, and on the wall behind the desk is the ceremonial shield presented by him to Lord Stamford. The Ethiopian flag draped over the Ante-Room door was, during the Emperor's lifetime, always flown at Dunham on his birthday.

Lord Stamford was a man of regular habits, and the route he trod each day to reach his desk is clearly marked by a track of threadbare carpet. At the far end of the desk, in neat piles, he kept copies of the *Altrincham Guardian* and the *Liverpool Post*, part of a massive collection of newspapers started before the First World War and housed mainly in the adjacent Ante-Room and, in the case of *The Times*, in the cellar. In the window is the *chaise-longue* on which the Earl would rest when not attending to business or his correspondence, and in

front of the fireplace is the leather chair where he would sit when talking with a friend or member of the family. He would not, however, have a telephone or a wireless in the room, and he never owned a television, which he considered bad for the eyes. If ever he particularly wanted to watch something, he would visit a friend in the village, sitting as far away from the screen as possible.

THE STUDY ANTE-ROOM

Before the First World War the Ante-Room was the office of the 9th Earl's private secretary, Captain Wood. It subsequently became a gunroom and is now used to show documents, photographs and family papers relating to the Booths and Greys and their estates.

On the mantelshelf is an 18th-century *Delftware box* and *two Chinese blue-and-white baluster vases*, Kangxi, early 18th-century. Above is a *Portrait of a Lady*, called Lady Jane Grey, although there is no accepted likeness of the Nine Days' Queen, and this is probably an 18th-century invention. The dress depicted in the portrait was replicated for the 10th Earl's sister, also Lady Jane, for her part in a procession of descendants of kings and queens at a London ball in 1919. She was the only one there with exactly the same name as her forebear. In the mahogany wall-case opposite the window is the illuminated pedigree of the 2nd Earl of Warrington.

THE SOUTH CORRIDOR (WEST)

Lord Stamford's newspapers spilled out into this section of the South Corridor and, like the rest, they were carefully monitored. One of his nephews once removed a single copy to wrap up his army boots; shortly after returning to barracks, he received a telephone call requesting its return.

The *bronze tripod-stands* on the window-sills are early 19th-century. Above the panelling to the left of the White Room door, are three portraits: the far one, by George Knapton (1698–1778), is of an unknown man; that in the middle is a copy of the Romney of *the Hon. and Rev. Anchitel Grey* in the Saloon, and the near one, from the studio of Peter Lely, is of an earlier *Anchitel Grey*, second son of the 1st Earl of Stamford.

THE WHITE ROOM

The 10th Earl gathered here the pictures he and his father had inherited relating to the White family of Selborne in Hampshire – hence the name of the room. Lord Stamford's grandmother, Harriet, was the daughter of the Rev. Francis Henry White and the great-niece of the most famous member of that family – the Rev. Gilbert White (1720–93). He was the author of *The Natural History and Antiquities of Selborne* – the most enduringly popular book ever written on natural history – and lived at The Wakes in Selborne, which is the subject of one of the pictures in the room. The pen-and-watercolour sketch of *The Hermitage* on the hillside above The Wakes, by Samuel Hieronymous Grimm, was done to be engraved for the frontispiece of White's book. An engraving of the only known portrait of *Gilbert White* – a tiny drawing now in the British Museum – hangs in the middle of the wall to the left of the entrance. Opposite are portraits by H. T. Schafer of the 9th Earl's parents, *Harriet White* and *the Rev. William Grey*, and over the fireplace are early 19th-century silhouettes of the sons of the Rev. Harry Grey, including the 8th Earl, whose photograph later in life hangs next to the window.

Before proceeding to the Kitchen Courtyard, please retrieve any coats or bags left on entering the house.

THE KITCHEN COURTYARD

The formal parterre depicted in Kip's engraving of 1697 was done away with by the 2nd Earl of Warrington to allow for the present domestic courtyard. Rooms associated with the laundry, dairy, kitchen and housekeeping are gathered around here, with the Kitchen itself in the range opposite the open archway. It was positioned apart from the main house to prevent fire and cooking smells from spreading.

THE SCULLERY

The Scullery, immediately adjoining the Kitchen, was intended for all parts of the cooking process which needed water. The fireplace also includes an oven for bread, which was baked here as well as in the bakehouse.

Electricity, piped hot and cold water and the most up-to-date fittings by Clements Jeakes & Co. of Great Russell Street, London were introduced when all the rooms in this range were overhauled in 1905–8. The sink opposite the window, in robust tin, was for washing pots and pans, whilst the ceramic one next to the Kitchen door was for preparing vegetables, which could be stored underneath. Timber sinks, for washing crockery and other comparatively delicate items, were replaced after the Second World War, but their associated wall-mounted drainer survives to the right of the window. The corridor leading under the fireplace arch gives access to a lavatory for the kitchen staff, also part of the Edwardian improvements.

THE KITCHEN

The structure of Lord Warrington's great kitchen survives more or less intact, apart from the stone-flagged floor, which was replaced by tiles in the early 20th century. Its high and ceilingless roof, together with the numerous windows, gave maximum ventilation to a space which, unlike now, would have been very hot and full of steam and smoke. The blocked windows on the right-hand wall indicate that the Kitchen was probably attached only at ground-floor level until the principal part of the house was rebuilt in the 1730s. The Gallery, which must have been added then, gives access to rooms once occupied by kitchen-maids, and would also have allowed the house steward, as well as Lord Warrington and his successors, to inspect the Kitchen without having to set foot down below.

FITTINGS

The Kitchen remained in use right up to the death of the 10th Earl in 1976, and the fixtures and fittings have been subjected to constant change, with little surviving from the early 18th century. Charcoal stoves have probably been removed from beneath the windows at the end of the room, and those in the far left-hand arch, with a cast-iron casing, are early 19th-century and were later converted to gas. Such stoves were used to cook sauces and other things that needed a gentle heat. Pans stood above the stove openings on triangular iron trivets, several examples of which can be seen.

The massive arch in the right-hand wall would have housed an open roasting range in the 18th

The Kitchen about 1883

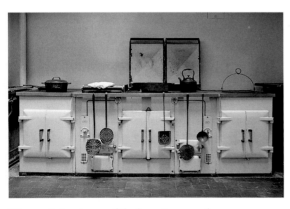

The 1936 Aga is one of the largest ever made

century, but by 1883, when the Kitchen was first photographed, it had been replaced with an enclosed version. The smoke jack, used for turning joints of meat in front of the open range, was at that time still in place and, although subsequently removed, its spits remain in the room, together with the copper drip-pan, which would have been placed under the cooking meat. Clements Jeakes & Co. changed the range again in the early 1900s, and in 1936 an Aga was installed. The Dunham Massey Aga is one of the earliest examples in existence – it had been invented only in the 1920s – and it is also one of the largest ever made: it has three double ovens, substantial simmering and hot plates, and plentiful additional warming space. To either side are domestic-scale gas cookers, that on the right being early 20th-century, whilst that on the left, which is still operational, was made in the 1930s. Between the arch and the door is an Edwardian patented 'hotbox', trumpeted as 'Invaluable for

Shooting and Boating Parties, Pic-Nics etc. etc.' and sufficiently insulated to allow food to continue cooking once placed inside.

The massive marble mortar to the left of the Scullery door, with its pestle held in place by an iron support, is probably that for which payment was made in 1790. In the nearby dresser is some of the pewter acquired and carefully checked by the meticulous 6th Earl, who instructed that it should be marked with his coronet, the initials S and W, for his earldoms of Stamford and Warrington, and the year. Most of it was acquired in 1819 and 1840. The 6th Earl also bought the kitchen table, stamped 1840, and probably much of the splendid *batterie de cuisine* of copper pans, kettles and moulds. Footmen could place trays on the shelf running along the near wall before taking them through to the old dining room.

Leave by the door to the right of the dresser.

THE CHEF'S ROOM

This was both a dry larder, for storing dry ingredients and prepared food, and the Pastry, as it was known in the 18th century. A meat safe survives, together with the large slate slab, on which pastry was made, and a long dresser for storage. The room is particularly well planned: from here the chef could reach the other larders and monitor activity in the Kitchen through the window in the side wall. The larders had to be kept cool – hence their northerly aspect and originally unglazed windows. It was probably to reduce the heat of the Kitchen flues that the unusual timber grilles were introduced between the three larders in 1832.

The Butler's Pantry

THE WET AND MEAT LARDERS

The slate-topped tables provided by Clements Jeakes & Co. and the earlier slate sinks on sandstone supports were intended for cleaning and salting raw meat and fish. Some meat would have been hung here ready for use, but most would have been kept in the adjoining Meat Larder, with its massive suspended rack, which was strong enough to support even carcasses of fallow deer. Game birds and meat in storage for a long period remained in the Game Larder (not open), which is attached to the rest of the range only at one corner, to ensure maximum ventilation and the lowest possible temperature.

By the door from the Wet Larder to the Chef's Room is a refrigerator supplied by Clements Jeakes & Co. in the early 1900s. The huge cheese press opposite the window was in the Dairy in 1905. Several bird cages, probably for parrots, are now stored in the Meat Larder, together with some tiered flower stands; those in basketware are perhaps survivors of the six acquired for the Entrance Gallery in 1822.

Retrace your steps and go straight across the Kitchen.

THE BUTLER'S PANTRY

The door from the Kitchen marks the beginning of the butler's domain, and to the right is his pantry, created by Compton Hall out of the former servants' hall. It survives exactly as fitted, with extensive cupboards for fine china and glass, drawers for table linen, ample space in the centre for setting trays, and drying and cleaning, and, under the windows, timber sinks for washing. Glass would have been washed separately from china to avoid grease, and was rinsed with specially collected soft rainwater, for which a third tap is provided over the right-hand sink. The butler communicated with the rest of the house and with the gate lodge via the switchboard for the internal telephone system, to the right of the entrance door. Above is an electric bell-board, which was the traditional way of communicating and which also informed him of anybody ringing at the front door.

A fire was always kept burning in the corner fireplace, and in his later years, when not entertaining, the 10th Earl would take tea here, sitting in a large Windsor chair on the right-hand side. The square iron to the left of the fireplace was used to smooth the billiard-table baize.

At the end of the passage is the sophisticated Servery.

THE SERVERY

The Jeakes & Co. cast-iron hot cupboard, which was heated by pipes from the kitchen range, kept food warm before it was passed by kitchen-maids through the serving hatch to footmen, to go on into the Dining Room. The platform is screened by oak panelling, both to shut out the Kitchen from the Dining Room, and to help enforce the division between the house and kitchen staff, which was rigidly maintained at Dunham before the Second World War.

Return to the Kitchen Courtyard and take the middle door in the right-hand range.

THE DAIRY AND MILK ROOM

The blackened appearance of these rooms results from the storage here of the large quantities of coke needed to fire the central-heating system installed by the 9th Earl in 1905–10. It is in marked contrast to the neat, whitewashed walls and scrubbed floors which would have been necessary when dairy products were made and stored here.

The higher room has always been called the Dairy, although it was more like a dairy scullery. The coppers flanking the range on the west wall (only one of which remains) would have been used for washing utensils, scalding cream and warming milk for cheese-making, and the large shelf opposite for storing cheese, butter and other dairy products.

The Milk Room, adjacent and set down a step, fulfilled the role more often associated with a dairy. Large, flat pans would have been placed on the shelves to allow milk to separate in the cool atmosphere, together with jugs of milk ready for use in the Kitchen, cream, cheeses, junkets and other milk puddings. The thick slate sinks in the bay with their worn marble backings would have been filled with water to stand jugs in and to help cool the air.

THE LAUNDRY

The Laundry, rebuilt in the 1720s, replaced a 17th-century complex to the north of the present Kitchen. Unlike most other restored laundries, where objects have been brought in from elsewhere, all the contents here are original to Dunham. Although Dunham's laundry was abandoned in the early 20th century in favour of a cottage laundry in the village, the rooms today are dressed as if they were still in use. Until the 7th Earl left in the 1850s, activity would have been almost constant when the family was in residence; in 1819 there were some 2,000 items of tableware, bedclothes and towels in the house, not including personal linen and cleaning cloths.

THE HEAD LAUNDRY-MAID'S BEDROOM

Situated to the right of the door from the courtyard, this is well placed to monitor access to the Laundry and is better fitted than were the rooms of the other laundry-maids (upstairs, not on view). Head laundry-maids were highly experienced, comparatively well paid and often from Ireland or Scotland, which were renowned for their laundering skills. In 1871 30-year-old Janet Milligan from Dumfries filled the post. As was usual with servants' bedrooms, the room also served as a store for surplus furniture.

THE DRY LAUNDRY

The Dry Laundry, rising through two storeys, was used for starching, ironing, folding and airing large quantities of household cotton and linen. Its two large windlasses, the overhead airing racks (or 'fleaks') operated by them, and a long work-table for ironing and folding – which, in use, would have been covered by blanketing and sheeting – were here by 1819. The 'Pagoda' stove by Thomas Bradford of Salford is later.

THE MANGLE ROOM

The massive box-mangle, which was in here by 1819, was used for smoothing out partially dried linen and not for wringing out water immediately after washing, as is often assumed. With great care, items would be wrapped around the wooden rollers before being turned under the box, which was given sufficient weight by being filled with stones. Turning was done by an odd-job man, who also operated the wheel of the pump to the right of the window, to provide water for the Laundry.

THE WASH-HOUSE

Prior to 1800, when this room was added, washing was undertaken in the present Dry Laundry, and drying in the Mangle Room. The new Wash-house was exceptionally well equipped, with the largest of the built-in coppers providing hot water via pipes and taps (now gone) to the rectangular wooden sinks opposite, and the others being used to boil whites after they had been scrubbed. Cold water was also piped to the sinks, which emptied into the open drain beneath. Slops from free-standing tubs would have been disposed of in the quarter-shaped stone cistern in the corner. From the 1860s an upright mangle was used to wring out the washing.

The door to the left of the entrance leads to what was the 'drying ground' (not open), where laundry would have been hung until only damp before being brought inside to be pressed or ironed, then folded and aired. In the 18th century washing was placed on lawns and hedges to dry, as can be seen clearly in Harris's *Bird's-eye View of Dunham from the North*, painted in 1751. By 1819 the hedges had given way to wire clothes lines.

Return to the Kitchen Courtyard and leave through the arch.

THE STABLES AND COACH-HOUSE

The coach-house and stable ranges, known as the North and South Stables, were probably completed in 1721 – the date on the Great Clock over the coach-house arch. As originally built, the South Stables were only half their present width, and may have been expanded by the 5th Earl of Stamford to accommodate his string of racehorses. Inside, there are fine stalls for the riding horses, and a smaller group of stalls for the cows which supplied the Dairy. There was also provision for cart-horses, and on the other side of the Moat is the simple square enclosure in which stallions were kept away from the mares. The spaces above the stalls, now occupied by the restaurant and its kitchen, would have been grooms' quarters and haylofts, while the

The North and South Stables

Armstrong Siddeley by Lady Stamford after the First World War to be taught driving and maintenance skills. He served Lord Stamford for 65 years and lies buried alongside his employer in the churchyard of St Mark's, Dunham Massey.

THE MILL

Situated beyond the South Stables and the foot of the moat which feeds it, this is the only part of 'Old' Sir George Booth's extensive building works to survive. It is said to have been built in 1616, perhaps on the site of the 'Pool Mill' listed in an account roll for 1380–1.

Corn was ground here until the mid-19th century, but virtually all that survives of the grinding equipment is the millstone, dated 1684, now outside the building. Everything else was removed in the 1860s when it was converted into a sawmill and workshop, perhaps because the corn mill across the meadow at Bollington was being rebuilt on a much larger scale. By the early 20th century the Mill had entirely fallen out of use, and the 9th Earl had a more efficient steam-powered sawmill set up in the estate yard, to the south of the park. Compton Hall restored the structure of the Mill, and in the late 1970s the water-wheel and the rest of the machinery were brought back to working order by Dr Cyril Boucher.

present shop fills the lower half of the racquets court created by Compton Hall for the 9th Earl in 1907–8.

Carriage horses, which needed space to move around because of their irregular exercise, were kept in loose boxes in the left-hand range of the North Stables, where the lavatories now are. There was direct access from here to the yard in front of the coach-houses, the massive arched doors of which are painted in Dunham blue. When the diarist Walter Aston visited Dunham in 1825, he wrote: 'We went through the Earl's Coach-Houses and saw seven Close Carriages of his, besides Landaus etc.' – a prodigious quantity.

The right-hand range of the North Stables originally housed the Brew-house and Bakehouse, detached from the Kitchen Courtyard as a precaution against fire. Between 1905 and 1910 Compton Hall created an up-to-date garage range, opening up the Brew-house to the yard to provide a wash for the cars and carriages. Beyond the Wash is the Chauffeur's Room (not open) and, in the adjoining coach-houses, garaging for three cars equipped with central heating, an inspection pit and electric light. Between the wars, the 10th Earl's two Armstrong Siddeleys were housed in what is now the ticket office, to be followed by a Morris Oxford, its green leather upholstery specially requested from Lord Nuffield. The single garage still contains Lord Stamford's dark green 1934 Morris 10 hp Dickey-Seater, generously loaned by Michael Lee. The cars were lovingly tended by the chauffeur, Piers Davenport, who was sent to

The Mill

THE GARDEN

HISTORY

The garden is dominated by the moat, which is first recorded in 1411, but is probably much older. By the 17th century the moat's defensive role had ceased, and although thereafter primarily decorative, it continued to provide fish for the Kitchen, 250 brace of trout being extracted in April 1823 alone. It is not clear whether the associated Mount was the site of a castle, but it certainly formed part of the garden created by 'Old' Sir George Booth at the beginning of the 17th century. It was still in its Jacobean state when van Diest and Knyff recorded the house and garden in 1697. As well as the clipped hedges and gabled summer-house of the prospect mount, these views show the 'Old but good gardens walled in' seen by Celia Fiennes the following year and the formal grass parterre and orangery to the west of the house, on the site of the current Kitchen Courtyard. They do not appear to show the bowling green mentioned in Henry Newcome's Diary in 1663, when it was in frequent use.

In the early 18th century the 2nd Earl of Warrington did away with the walled enclosures of the old house and included most of the land in his ambitious scheme for the park, the results of which can be seen in the four bird's-eye views executed by John Harris the Younger in 1751 and now hanging in the Great Gallery. Lord Warrington laid out two

Van Diest's view of around 1697 shows the garden created by 'Old' Sir George Booth in the early 17th century, with its walled formal gardens and prospect mount beside the moat

Dunham from the south-east in 1751, showing the parterres laid out by the 2nd Earl of Warrington under the east front

parterres beneath the east front – one in the form of a maze – and he rendered the Mount fashionable by presenting it as a series of diminishing turf terraces, topped by a vast gilded urn. He also constructed a curiously shaped productive walled garden near the house and another, much larger version, with formal paths and an obelisk, beyond the park wall.

The 4th Earl and Countess of Stamford seem to have changed little, and the 5th Earl initially devoted his energy to the landscape at Enville. It was probably not until he was updating Dunham's south front in 1789–90 that he turned his attention to the immediate setting of the house, creating a garden of flowing lawns and naturalistic planting which forms the basis of what is seen today. According to J. Aikin's *Description of the Country ... around Manchester* (1795): 'The ground around this house has lately been laid out in ornamental manner with shrubberies, flower-beds, etc.' In 1792 and 1795 Lord Stamford bought purple beech, two survivors of which can still be seen near the Orangery.

Interest in the garden continued to be strong throughout the first half of the 19th century. Large numbers of plants were supplied by the burgeoning horticultural nurseries of the time, and others were grown from seed, including two Sugar Pines (*Pinus lambertiana*) from California in 1836. In 1831 George Harry, Lord Grey of Groby (eldest son of the 6th Earl) was able to mark off over 650 trees, shrubs and flowers as being at Dunham in his copy of Loudon's *Hortus Britannicus*, and an early 19th-century document lists 35 different roses 'For the Earl of Stamford at Dunham Massey'. All the new introductions were displayed in the Pleasure Ground (as the decorative part of the garden has been known since the late 18th century), which was maintained to a very high standard, with a large number of extra staff being drafted in every autumn to keep the paths and lawns free of leaves.

The 7th Earl, who succeeded in 1845, had an enormous enthusiasm for gardening, and by 1853 expenditure on the garden had doubled. He introduced fashionable island beds, constructed the Bark House, and placed a bridge across the moat. Because the Earl was increasingly absent from Dunham and less careful about his affairs, however, activity slowed down, and standards began to slip. John Bancroft, then one of the under-gardeners, wrote in 1906:

It is over 70 years since I first worked in the gardens, being now in my eightieth year... But alas what a

In 1883 the lawn was ornamented with island beds. The Bark House has since been moved from beside the Orangery to the front of the Well House

difference took place when the late Earl had come to age [1848]. I witnessed a festival of drink.... Mr Wilcox the head gardener influencing the men to drink by a vulgar expression not fit to mention.

In the late 19th century the garden was reasonably well maintained in spite of the absence of the family, but no significant alterations were made until after the 9th Earl inherited in 1905. A plan drawn up in March 1909 shows that a square grid of paths, in place of serpentines, had begun to be developed in front of the Orangery, and that most of the island beds had been removed. The 9th Earl also created a parterre on the north front and a rose garden beyond the canal, the latter reflecting Lady Stamford's particular fondness for roses. During the summer, heavy tubs planted with geraniums were placed at the corners of paths, and, until the Second World War, badminton and tennis courts and a bowling green were set out on the lawns, and boats placed on the moat for use during house parties and visits by Lady Jane Turnbull and her children. Garden parties were held for charity, particularly the Red Cross and, every four years, for all the tenants – farmers one day and cottage tenants the next. Lord Stamford, his mother and sister and any other dignitaries stood by the garden gate to shake hands with all those entering, and there were marquees in front of the Orangery, a brass band and plentiful supplies of lemonade and ices, but very definitely no alcohol.

During the Second World War all the gardeners except Gilbert Gilles, the head gardener, were called up, and a somewhat unsuccessful attempt was made to turn the lawns over to growing potatoes. The garden staff shrank from eleven in the 1930s to two in the post-war years, and it was not until the estate had been bequeathed to the National Trust that work began on restoring and developing the garden to its present state. By then, much of the detail had been lost, and the decision was

The north parterre

taken to develop new schemes in sympathy with the surviving essence of the garden as a pleasure ground, but not restricted to the use of historic plants. The restoration, masterminded by the National Trust's former Head of Gardens, John Sales, and carried out by a dedicated team of five gardeners, has made Dunham amongst the best-stocked gardens in the country, despite poor and extremely acid soil. The garden contains a remarkable variety of ground-cover planting and waterside plants, a unique range of azaleas and good collections of hydrangeas, skimmias and other uncommon trees and shrubs.

TOUR OF THE GARDEN

The tour starts at the entrance gate and follows a roughly clockwise route.

The present garden lies to the east and north of the house and is entered through a corner of the garden wood, which has only been fully incorporated into the garden for about twenty years. Around the entrance mock orange, deutzia and roses are underplanted with a range of ground-cover plants, including forms of hardy geranium and comfrey and the green-flowered *Tellima grandiflora*. Following the path to the left, dog's-tooth violets give an exotic display of spring colour, and under the trees, at the same time of year, is a mass of bluebells among common yellow azaleas. Against the late 18th-century ha-ha wall is a stream which was once used to grow watercress for the house, and now has extensive and lush plantings alongside it of moisture-loving hostas, skunk cabbage and shuttlecock ferns.

Continuing to the left, the path goes through a belt of hollies and rhododendrons marking the old garden boundary and emerges on the lawns which have been such an important part of the garden since the 1790s. The borders near the house have been planted boldly with velvety reds, strong blues and deep purples, the plants including roses, peonies, delphiniums and day lilies. As well as a tall Swamp Cypress (*Taxodium distichum*) growing improbably within a few feet of the house, several unusual young trees are beginning to articulate the lawns. These include the summer-flowering *Tetradium daniellii*, the free-flowering dogwood, *Cornus* 'Eddie's White Wonder', and a

curious form of the acacia, *Robinia pseudoacacia* 'Unifoliola'.

The north parterre, between the house and the moat, retains the flanking hedges of Golden Yew, paved paths and formal beds of the Edwardian lay-out, although the beds have been augmented. They contain pansies and wallflowers in spring, then lobelias, variegated pelargoniums and verbenas, and follow a colour scheme of yellows with strong blue or purple for contrast. The four ball-shaped topiary pieces have been formed out of the rare evergreen oak, *Quercus phillyreoïdes*. Beyond the far hedge is the Mount, which is shaded by false acacias, first planted by the 6th Earl, together with laburnums, in 1821. The Mount was probably reduced to a gentle grassy hillock from its former eminence by the 5th Earl in the 1790s and has been kept deliberately simple, cool and green with hardy ferns, ivies and climbing hydrangeas as ground cover.

Returning to the lawns by the moat edge, you can once again see the Orangery. This handsome red-brick building, enhanced by climbing roses of the 19th-century noisette type, was probably constructed in the second half of the 18th century after the 2nd Earl of Warrington's walled garden had been cleared from the site. Its slate roof replaced one of glass in the early 20th century, and the resultant challenge of dim light has been met with abutilons on the walls and, in large terracotta pots, *Abutilon* 'Cynthia Pike', grown as standards among white *Impatiens*. Outside in summer stand clipped myrtles in tubs, the façade being framed by trees and shrubs chosen for their foliage contrast. The little fountain pond has been left entirely unadorned, as was probably intended when it was constructed in the early 19th century. Behind the Orangery is an exhibition on the history of the garden and its development.

The Bark House was moved from the side of the Orangery by the 9th Earl to the front of the early 18th-century Well House, in which water was originally pumped into a cistern and then fed by gravity to the ground floor of the house. In the mid-19th century a more efficient pumping system was installed in the Mill, capable of running continuously. Just beyond the Bark House a path leads to the head of the canal, which feeds the

Dunham is famous for the azaleas bred by the late Denny Pratt

moat. The sunny borders along here include brooms, romneyas, *Clerodendrum bungei* and *Viburnum plicatum* 'Mariesii', and there is a fine specimen of *Enkianthus campanulatus*. The herbaceous planting against the canal combines waterside irises and peonies for June with day lilies for July and August. This area was probably first brought into the garden by the 6th Earl, who in 1821 bought large numbers of shrubs from Caldwell's Nursery.

In the centre of the North Avenue, and in view from the house, is a row of graves of the favoured dogs of the family, including 'Pugg, als. old Vertue, who dyed February 17th, 1702' – the dog so favoured by the 2nd Earl of Warrington that he had it immortalised in a painting. A path, known as Emily's Walk after the daughter of a former head gardener, leads back through an archway of *Rosa filipes* and old hybrid rhododendrons to the canal path. At the opposite end a hedge of *Osmanthus heterophyllus* separates the canal path from the Edwardian rose garden, abandoned during the Second World War. Its purple beech hedges, left unclipped, have grown into a sombre cathedral, in which nothing thrives but moss, and rather than destroy a tranquil and cool retreat, it has instead been developed as a moss garden – one of only two in the country.

Returning again to the lawn, you will find a path that leads past several specimen trees. They include variegated, red and holm oaks that have been here since at least 1831, and a cork oak planted by the 6th Earl two years later. The tulip tree was probably planted to replace those lost in the 1890s and recorded at the time as among the largest in the country. The long border against the east boundary wall contains an interesting mixture of shrubs dominated by hybrids derived from *Rhododendron yakushimanum*, cultivars of the small lacecap *Hydrangea serrata* and skimmia species. In the wall at the far end is an early 18th-century wrought-iron gate probably made by Robert Bakewell, which incorporates the three boars' heads of the Booth coat of arms. Further round the lawn, past a group of cherries underplanted with rhododendrons, is a fine clump of *Magnolia tripetala*, which bears huge, parchment-coloured and fragrant flowers in June. Next to this a new border has been planted with a variety of unusual herbaceous plants and shrubs, and beyond are recently planted hybrid rhododendrons.

A rustic bridge on the left leads to the garden wood, the path emerging in a recently created glade of acers. To the right, in spring, is the star-turn of Dunham's streamside planting: *Meconopsis × sheldonii*, of a quality and intensity of blue seldom seen. Following the stream to the left, the hydrangea corner is reached, containing a wide range mostly of the species and their forms. The large *H. heteromalla* and *H. aspera* forms, including *H. a. sargentiana* and *a. villosa,* have been interspersed with bamboos and grasses for contrast, and the smaller kinds, including the excellent *H. arborescens* ssp. *radiata*, with grasses and sedges. Amongst the hydrangeas, in the summer, the dramatic giant lily *Cardiocrinum giganteum* has formed a sizeable colony to great effect. Further into the garden wood deciduous azaleas are the theme. Dunham holds an important collection of late-flowering and fragrant hybrids developed by the late Denny Pratt, using *Rhododendron*

Gunnera thrives in the moist conditions of the Bog Garden

occidentale, *R. atlanticum*, *R. bakeri*, *R. prunifolium* and *R. viscosum*, sometimes with *R. luteum* or Ghent hybrids. Mr Pratt, who was a remarkable plantsman and had lectured on botany at Liverpool University, died in 1988, and some of his latest crosses subsequently came to Dunham Massey to join those already here.

Throughout the garden wood, seedling trees and undergrowth have been thinned to make space for planting and to reveal some of the fine specimen trees, including the uncommon Corstorphine Plane, *Acer pseudoplatanus* 'Corstorphinense', and the Altrincham Maple, *Acer pseudoplatanus* 'Brilliantissimum', with yellow and pink spring foliage respectively. The circuit of the garden ends in an open area near the house, where roses tolerant of the light acid soil thrive.

THE PARKS AND ESTATE

THE OLD PARK

The Old Park is of ancient origin, being first recorded in 1362, and it still contains a few venerable oaks from medieval plantings as well as the herd of fallow deer, which was probably established here at an early stage. Little, however, is known of the development of the Old Park before the late 17th century, when the 2nd Earl of Warrington began his prodigious planting programme. He had inherited in 1694, and by 1697, when van Diest and Knyff recorded the landscape immediately around the house, two avenues had been planted to the south, and one to the north. Lord Warrington subsequently had another four avenues laid out to the south, creating a total of six which fan out from

a D-shaped clearing at the end of the south lawn. Between the avenues, blocks of woodland were planted – oak, beech, lime and chestnut predominating – and whilst some were dense, with walks and rides cutting through to create geometric patterns, others were more open and apparently random, to give the impression of informality. The whole was interspersed with sheets of water – regular and irregular in outline – as well as park buildings, statuary and other sculpture, and a serpentine path gave a circuit route for pedestrians, from which the best views within the park and across the surrounding countryside could be enjoyed.

Old Man's Pool in the Old Park

The Langham Grove, according to the inscription on the obelisk put up at its centre to commemorate the family of the 2nd Earl's mother, was planted in 1714 and the brick deer barn, for the winter feeding of the deer, has a beam incised '1740'. Otherwise, the only specific dates known for the park are those for the encircling wall, which was begun at the Smithy Gate 'Upon St James's Day' in 1748. When it was finished, three years and over two miles later, the by-then elderly Lord Warrington obviously considered his park to be complete and commissioned the series of bird's-eye views from John Harris the Younger, which forms such a remarkable visual record of what had been achieved and what, to a substantial degree, survives today.

Lord Warrington's park was intended to express his power and taste, to show his patriotism in growing timber for the future needs of a maritime nation, and to be a source of profit as well as pleasure. Profit was particularly important to Lord Warrington, having inherited a near-bankrupt estate, and he is reputed to have justified the massive scale of his planting by stating to critics: 'Gentlemen, you may think it strange that I do these things; but I have the inward satisfaction in my own breast; the benefit of posterity; and my survivors will receive more than double the profit, than by any other method I could possibly take for their interest.' In 1762 it was estimated that there were 31,000 trees within the park wall. After 1792 timber and bark sales consistently brought in over 20 per cent of the estate's total income.

The Old Park was left largely intact by the more informal style introduced by 'Capability' Brown in the mid-18th century, with the exception of the area immediately around the house, which the 5th Earl laid out as an informal garden in the 1790s. He had also created a new drive (known as Ash Walk) in 1779, removed the more regular stretches of water within the park, and disposed of much of the sculpture, including the statue of Hercules from the Island Pool in 1783. The only other changes have been brought about by the need to manage the growing timber and by the natural demise of trees. Ongoing replanting is intended to perpetuate the layout recorded so vividly in Harris's views.

The 2nd Earl of Warrington created a series of six great avenues which cut through his new plantations to the south of the house; by John Harris (Great Gallery)

THE NEW PARK

The New Park, which lies to the north of the B5160, is a golf course, and access is possible only by the public footpaths, which run along the principal drives.

Almost immediately after Lord Warrington daughter, Lady Stamford, inherited in 1758, she set about transforming Dunham's other park, known until the mid-18th century as the Higher Park. As shown in the Harris views, this area had probably not changed significantly since its foundation at much the same time as the Old Park (it is first mentioned separately in 1434). In 1759 the Countess had the Green Walk laid out at the southern end as a carriage drive to the church at Bowdon. By 1765, the park had changed sufficiently to gain its present name – the New Park. The work may have been carried out by 'Capability' Brown himself: the planting was very much in his style, and the beech-covered mound at the north end is typical of his artificial earthworks. The 4th Earl of Stamford recommended Brown for a royal appointment, which suggests that the Earl or his wife was a patron, and Brown is not thought to have been employed elsewhere by the family.

*Dunham New Park in 1767, by Anthony Devis
(Rose Gallery)*

Although some villas were developed along the southern edge around 1900, the New Park was maintained as a park until it was requisitioned at the beginning of the Second World War: from 1942 to 1946 it was used as a prisoner-of-war camp, primarily for Germans. With their closely shaven heads and highly polished boots, the prisoners were well known in the area, and Lord Stamford, who employed some of them in his kitchen garden, is said to have cycled up to the camp on Sundays to practise his 'High' German. After the war a golf course was developed on the New Park, and an area of land was compulsorily purchased for a covered reservoir. These changes inevitably damaged the planting, although the Trust hopes to carry out some restoration over the next few years.

The introduction in 1773 of a passenger service on the Duke of Bridgewater's newly completed canal opened up Dunham's parks to the people of Manchester, and by the mid-19th century, with the train also available, large numbers were visiting every year. G. R. Gott wrote in his *Pictorial History of Manchester* (1843):

… Dunham Park is a spot to which almost every man, woman and child in Manchester, who can afford the means of conveyance, pays one or more visits every season. Whitsuntide, however, the greatest holiday festival throughout the year in the north of England, is the principal period for visiting…. On a single afternoon during last Whitsuntide, although the weather was far from favourable, the number of visitors in the park was not less than twenty thousand.

The Old Park continues to draw visitors from near and far. Yet it is a peaceful place, a haven for wildlife, and an important nature conservation site, now designated a Site of Special Scientific Interest. Continual management since medieval times as pasture-woodland, which was the natural habitat of lowland Britain before the onset of agriculture, has made it the only site in the North West with a significant number of very old trees. These support a complex and fragile ecosystem which is exceptionally rich in dead-wood beetles: 181 species have been recorded, including nine of the most threatened in the country, and twelve not known anywhere further north. The deer are a vital part of the equation – a rare forest dung beetle is associated with them – and in order to protect both them and the beetle fauna, certain areas of the park have been designated sanctuaries which visitors are asked not to enter. There is a small exhibition on the beetle fauna of the park in the 18th-century slaughterhouse, off the South Avenue, a rare surviving example of a building in which deer carcasses would have been hung after being culled.

THE ESTATE

Apart from the Roman road (now the A56) to the west of the parks and some Bronze Age barrows to the south of the Old Park, there is scant archaeological evidence for the ancient history of the estate. What is seen today has developed out of a traditional medieval arrangement of castle, manor house, village and outlying hamlets, with fields dedicated to arable strip-farming near to habitation, and pasture interspersed with heath and low-level wetland, known in Cheshire as moss, beyond. Few buildings survive from this time, with the notable exception of the White Cottage at Little Bollington, of *c.* 1500, and although timber-framing and thatch continued to predominate until well into the 19th century, all new building from about 1700 was in brick and slate. Some fine examples survive from the time of the 2nd Earl of Warrington, including the handsome Manor Farm

The octagonal dovecote in the Home Farm is painted in the crimson estate livery

The field system which had developed out of enclosure remained largely unaltered until the late 19th century, with the exception of the area near Altrincham, and especially on the elevated and airy Downs, which began to be developed as villas for the prosperous merchants of Manchester from about 1850. The 7th Earl, being an absentee, was not greatly concerned about the impact of this on the house and parks, unlike his grandfather, and he spent little of the profits on the remainder of the estate. By the 1870s many of the farm buildings were in a very poor state, and the tenants were in no position to cope with the agricultural depression of the period. The nettle was grasped only after Lord Stamford's death in 1883, when the trustees managing the estate decided upon a drastic course of action – wholesale conversion to dairy production in order to benefit from the huge demand from Manchester and Warrington. Between 1889 and 1917 virtually every farmhouse and all the farm buildings were renovated or rebuilt in the 'Stamford' design drawn up by the estate office, which includes the use of bright red machine-brick surrounds to the windows and doors. At the same time the hotch-potch of small fields, which had developed over several hundred years, was swept away with most of the hedgerows, and replaced with a grid of fields bounded by quickthorn.

The succession of the 9th Earl in 1905 speeded up the process of improvement. Several new cottages were constructed to replace those no longer deemed fit for habitation, and the rest were modernised. All received water closets, proper drainage and modern cooking ranges, and, in time, electricity and bathrooms were also installed.

The estate now comprises just over 3,000 acres – a substantial area in today's terms, but considerably reduced from the 31,000 acres in eight counties held by the 7th Earl in 1873. It is a working estate, and the twenty farms and 100 cottages, which are identifiable by their bright crimson paint and neat cleft-oak fences, are all let to private tenants.

at Dunham Woodhouses and a pair of cottages dated 1730 at Dunham Town, but the 6th Earl of Stamford's Home Farm complex of 1822 is the most impressive range of buildings outside the park wall. At the centre of the quadrangle of farm buildings is a pretty octagonal dovecote, its interior virtually complete. The nearby houses at right-angles to each other were intended for the farmer and the Earl's steward; the aviary adjoining the farmhouse, of c.1830, was constructed either for pheasants or fighting cocks.

The medieval farmland was gradually enclosed between the 15th and the 18th centuries, and by the early 19th century all of the wetland except that at Carrington, a mile to the north, had also been enclosed. The estate was largely devoted to arable farming, with oats and barley – for cattle feed, barley bread and brewing – predominating, but other crops were grown as well, including hemp and flax for the domestic textile industry, which flourished in the area until the late 18th century. The only other industries on the estate were brick-making and a small-scale salt-works at Dunham Woodhouses, which had existed since at least 1633 and survived until the 1770s.

THE BOOTHS AND THE GREYS

THE DE MASSEYS AND EARLY BOOTHS

The history of Dunham has been marked by repeated, often dramatic, changes in the fortunes of its owners ever since the Saxon freeman, Alweard, was displaced by a Norman knight, Hamo de Massey, in the 11th century. A long line of de Masseys subsequently held Dunham, all with the Christian name of Hamo. By the early 14th century the estate was in severe decline, and through financial necessity the last Sir Hamo de Massey was forced to divide Dunham. It was not until the early 15th century that the manor was reunited, by Sir Robert Booth.

The Booths were already a well-established family in the locality, living at Barton-on-Irwell (now part of Manchester) from the late 13th century. In the 15th and 16th centuries they provided a remarkable number of prominent churchmen: Sir Robert's brothers, William and Laurence, were both Archbishop of York, and later generations produced bishops, archdeacons, deans and other clerics.

Archaeology has failed to find any evidence of a Norman motte and bailey at Dunham, but there was certainly a house here by 1410/11, when it contained, 'A certain hall with a high chamber … a chapel and other small chambers adjoining', as well as a treasury, a kitchen and a stable. However, it was probably in a poor state, as a ruined dovecote is also mentioned, and Sir Robert Booth probably resided mainly at Bollin Hall, near Wilmslow, which his wife had inherited. He and his son were buried in the church at Wilmslow, but in 1484 his grandson, George Booth, was interred at Bowdon, perhaps indicating that he was living at nearby Dunham Massey. By the late 16th century Dunham was undoubtedly the family's principal residence.

'OLD' AND 'YOUNG' SIR GEORGE BOOTH

'Old' Sir George Booth, as he has become known to distinguish him from his grandson, was thirteen when he inherited in 1579, and as a ward of the Crown he was placed under the guardianship of Elizabeth I's favourite, the Earl of Leicester. Two years previously he had been married to Jane Carrington of Carrington, who brought him a considerable fortune, and on his coming-of-age in 1587 he was able to use his great wealth to improve and expand his already substantial estates. Sir George purchased land to the enormous value of £25,000 and, probably around 1600, 'Builded

'Old' Sir George Booth – 'free, grave, godley, brave Booth, flower of Cheshire', who rebuilt Dunham around 1600. The mill is all that survives from his era (South Corridor)

'Young' Sir George Booth, who created the Chapel and led Booth's Rebellion in support of the exiled Charles II in 1659; after Sir Peter Lely (Crimson Staircase)

three parte of Dunham house, all his barnes, Milles, gardens and Stables and at every other demaine house putt some parte thereof in reasonable repaier...'. The van Diest and Knyff views of 1697 record his work, which, apart from the Mill, was all swept away in the early 18th century.

'Old' Sir George had been knighted in 1597 and was created a baronet in 1611 by James I. He was dubbed 'free, grave, godley, brave Booth, flower of Cheshire' by a Puritan pamphleteer and was highly influential in the county, serving as Sheriff twice and as Justice of the Peace and Deputy Lieutenant for nearly sixty years. As a 'good church Puritan' he threw in his lot with Parliament on the outbreak of the Civil War in 1642, but he did not support the abolition of the monarchy or the execution of the King, and by the time of his death ten years later, at the age of 86, he had become disillusioned with Cromwell's rule.

'Young' Sir George Booth, 2nd Bt, who inherited from his grandfather, also supported Parliament, for which he raised forces in 1642–3, and he married as his second wife, Lady Elizabeth Grey, the daughter of another prominent Parliamentarian, the 1st Earl of Stamford, whose great-great-grandson was to inherit Dunham. He was thus the brother-in-law of the regicide Lord Grey of Groby, but, unlike Lord Grey, he did not support the execution of the King and was expelled from Parliament in 1648 for opposing the trial. His uncle, Colonel Sir John Booth, was twice imprisoned for actively conspiring against Parliament and on the third occasion, in 1651, he was only extricated from the Tower of London thanks to the good name and money of his 85-year-old father.

'Young' Sir George was elected to Parliament again in 1654 and 1656, as one of the members for Cheshire, but devoted himself primarily to the continued improvement of Dunham Massey, adding the south range and in 1655 creating the Chapel out of two rooms behind the Great Hall. Sir George became increasingly incensed at Cromwell's authoritarianism and at the marginalising of the Presbyterian interest. He wanted Parliament to be elected freely, with its members, as he wrote in 1659, allowed to 'as freely sit, without awe, or force or souldiary'. He had received overtures from the exiled Charles II as early as 1654 and in July 1659 he agreed to act as commander-in-chief of the north-western forces in a rising intended to erupt throughout the country. He was described to the King at the time as a 'Presbyterian in opinion, yet so moral a man ... I think your Majesty may safely [depend] on him and his promises which are considerable and hearty'. Sir George initially met with considerable success, gaining control of south Lancashire and all of Cheshire before the Commonwealth forces under Colonel Lambert could gather. When they did, Booth was easily driven back to Winnington Bridge, on the River Weaver near Northwich, and was defeated in a skirmish there on 19 August. Sir George fled disguised as a woman, but was apprehended at Newport Pagnell in Buckinghamshire, his large shoes and need of a barber having aroused the suspicions of an innkeeper. At gun point 'Mistress Dorothy' admitted to being 'that unfortunate gentleman, Sir George Booth' and was transported to London, remaining in the Tower until

February 1660. He was rewarded for his efforts by Charles II, who created him Baron Delamer of Dunham Massey in 1661, and by Parliament, which voted him £20,000, only half of which he took. Under the new King, however, the Presbyterian interest lost most of its national influence, and in the North West the Earl of Derby, who had been subordinate to Booth in 1659, reasserted his family's local pre-eminence. Lord Delamer retired to Dunham, his resources, pride and political influence all severely dented.

HENRY BOOTH, 1ST EARL OF WARRINGTON

Henry Booth was, if anything, more uncompromisingly moralistic and Presbyterian than his father, the 1st Lord Delamer, and after being elected to Parliament in 1678, he became a thorn in the side of the King and his ministers. He spoke strongly for the exclusion from the throne of the King's younger brother, the Catholic Duke of York, sought legislation to punish MPs who had received court bribes, and made a speech in 1680 berating the infamous Judge Jeffreys for his arbitrariness, and for having 'behaved himself more like a "Jack-Pudding" than with that gravity that beseems a judge'. In September 1682 he further taunted the King by entertaining the Duke of Monmouth as part of the Duke's attempt to promote himself amongst Protestants as an alternative heir to the throne. When Monmouth made a near-regal progress from Nantwich to Chester, Booth went ahead of him, 'well mounted and armed, finely habited with rich furniture on his horse, several led horses and servants going before'. The party was met at Dunham on 14 September by as many tenants as Booth could muster, and Lord Delamer laid on lavish entertainment, as did Booth himself at his own house, Mere Hall, the following day.

It is hardly surprising, in the light of these events, that Booth was suspected of involvement in the 1683 Rye House Plot against the lives of Charles II and his brother James, and in July he was arrested and placed in the Tower of London. The case being unproven, he was released after seven months, but he was in the Tower again in July 1685, following Monmouth's rebellion, although he had taken no

The monument to the 1st Earl and Countess of Warrington in Bowdon church

part in it, and in December he was charged with High Treason. Having succeeded his father in the Barony of Delamer in August 1684, he was entitled to be tried in the House of Lords, but as Parliament was not sitting, his case was heard in Westminster Hall before a jury of 27 specially appointed peers. His judge was none other than Jeffreys, whom he had so vociferously attacked six years previously, and Delamer, conducting his own defence, was fortunate that the chief witness for the prosecution was easily proved to be unreliable. On hearing of the unanimous verdict of not guilty, the widow of Lord Russell, who had been executed following the Rye House Plot, wrote: 'I do bless God that he has caused some stop to be put to the shedding of blood in this poor land.'

Lord Delamer bided his time at Dunham Massey, working on a treatise of advice to his children, until the birth of a son to James II in October 1688 prompted action. Delamer met the Earls of Devonshire and Danby at Whittington in Derbyshire, where the three 'privately concerted the plan of the revolution'. On 15 November he gathered his supporters at Warrington, Manchester and Ashton-under-Lyne, and the next day addressed his tenants on Bowdon Downs before marching south to join the Protestant Prince of Orange, who had claimed the throne. On 17 December Lord Delamer was sent, with the Marquess of Halifax and the Earl of Shrewsbury, to advise James II to quit London, which advice he took. The King later conceded that 'the Lord Delamer whom he had used ill, had treated him with much more regard than the other two lords, to whom he had been kind and from whom he might better have expected it'.

Delamer was showered with appointments by the victorious Prince of Orange, now William III, becoming Lord Lieutenant of Cheshire in place of the Earl of Derby, a Privy Counsellor and Chancellor of the Exchequer. However, he quarrelled with his colleagues in the Treasury and was not suitably diplomatic with the King, being, as a contemporary poet put it, 'Fit to assist to pull a tyrant down, But not to please a Prince that mounts the throne'. In March 1690 he was sacked as Chancellor of the Exchequer and in recompense was granted the Earldom of Warrington and a pension of £2,000, little of which was ever paid. With no prospect of another government post, he returned to Dunham and gathered together his speeches and writings for publication. His beloved wife, Mary Langham, whom he termed 'The greatest blessing man did e'er enjoy', died in 1691, and Lord Warrington followed her in January 1694 after an eventful, but comparatively short, life – he was only 42.

GEORGE BOOTH, 2ND EARL OF WARRINGTON

The estate inherited by the 2nd Earl of Warrington was severely encumbered by debt. His father and grandfather had both paid a heavy toll for their involvement in the politics of the period, and by 1688 the sum owing amounted to about £50,000. Lady Warrington, according to her son, was forced to borrow from servants 'and even what little pocket-money my sister and I had', and the 1st Earl 'could never spare money for any sort of furniture … so that there was only the little Dining Room with old moath-eaten Turkey work chairs for company to dine in'. There were mortgages, unpaid marriage portions, debts to tradesmen, election managers and even undertakers, and in some cases servants had not received their wages for many years. Dunham Massey Hall was in 'rotten condition and very barely furnished with worn out goods', and the whole estate 'in the utmost disorder for want of repair'. It is little wonder, in the face of all this, that the 1st Earl had been seen 'aweeping from the greatness of his debts'.

The nineteen-year-old 2nd Earl realised that drastic action was needed if the estate was to remain in the family. Unlike his predecessors, he avoided public service, stating that it 'must necessarily be the absolute ruine of our family', and devoted himself instead to the improvement of the estate, shrewd investment and the paying or avoidance of debt. So single-minded was he that he even tried to conceal his father's Will, with its over-generous bequests to his brothers and sisters, and, as he wrote to his brother Henry in 1722, he felt driven 'to make money … the chief view in marriage'. In 1702 he secured a £20,000 dowry by marrying Mary Oldbury, the daughter of a London merchant, and by 1715, with 'a great deal of care and pain', the bulk of the estate's debts had been discharged.

In other respects, Lady Warrington proved a far from perfect match for the Earl, who as early as 1711 was complaining of her 'sower dogged temper', lack of conversation, and language which 'don't become a virtuous woman'. A contemporary described her as 'a limber, dirty fool', and she is said to have enjoyed humiliating her husband; tipping her coachman to overtake him on the way back from the Knutsford Races, upsetting the stalls at Altrincham's fair by driving through at breakneck speed, and attending athletic games where she would 'crack rude jokes with the young men'. Following the birth of their only child, Mary, in 1704, the couple 'lived in the same house as absolute strangers to each other at bed and board' until the Countess's death in 1740, after 38 years of loveless marriage. It is perhaps not surprising that the articulate Earl was driven to write a treatise on the desirability of divorce for incompatibility of temper, publishing it anonymously the year before Lady Warrington died.

Lord Warrington's matrimonial difficulties did not distract him from his principal aim in life, and during his long tenure of the estate he invested in a massive store of silver, which gave security, as well as showing his good taste and his ability to support the dignity of an earldom, unlike his father. He began collecting almost immediately upon inheriting and consistently patronised leading Huguenot goldsmiths, who offered both the best quality and value for money, as well as sharing his own Protestant faith. He was also a shrewd collector of furniture and paintings, obtaining such superb pieces as the *Guercino Allegory*, the Hall overmantel by Boujet, and, perhaps most impressive of all, the Grinling Gibbons carving of the

The 2nd Earl of Warrington with his only child and heir, Lady Mary Booth; by Michael Dahl (Queen Anne Room)

The Warrington heraldic boars appear on the massive silver wine cistern, which was made by Philip Rollos in 1701 for the 2nd Earl (Rose Room)

Crucifixion, which the Earl set up like an altarpiece in his inner sanctum, the Library.

It was probably not until most of the debt had been cleared in 1715 that Lord Warrington began completely reconstructing the house and outbuildings. The work was carried out by the otherwise little-known architect John Norris, and almost certainly began with the two stable blocks, probably completed in 1721, before progressing to the Kitchen and domestic quarters, and finishing, in the 1730s, with the main part of the house. On visiting Dunham in 1735, John Dodd referred to building

being in progress, and payments were made to Norris 'about the new building' up to 1740. Lord Warrington then turned his attention to completing the structural elements of the remarkable park, which he had begun planting in the 1690s. The laying of the final bricks of the park wall in 1751 seems to have marked for him the conclusion of his efforts to turn around the fortunes of the entire estate, and that year he commissioned the bird's-eye views in which the results were so proudly displayed. On his death seven years later, Dunham passed to his daughter, the Countess of Stamford, supported by a healthy income and investments, the house well-furnished, and everything in excellent order. Ever mindful of economy and suspicious of public display, the Earl directed that his body should be buried decently, 'but very privately and with as small expence as maybe', and that there should be no mourning, sermon or monument.

LADY MARY BOOTH

The 2nd Earl of Warrington's views on divorce were unconventional and ahead of their time, and so too was his attitude towards inheritance. Having striven so long and hard to put the estate on a sound financial footing, he considered himself to have 'purchased rather than inherited what I have;

Lady Mary Booth and her husband, the 4th Earl of Stamford (Tea Room)

consequently my daughter has rights before any other to reap the fruits'. Thus Dunham did not pass with the barony of Delamer (the Earldom died with Lord Warrington) to his cousin and heir-male, Nathaniel, but to his only daughter, Lady Mary Booth, who, unusually for the time, was in absolute control of her own affairs in spite of being married. Lord Warrington ensured this by leaving the estate in trust for her benefit rather than to her outright, and as he had carefully coached her in matters of management, she was able to deal personally with such complicated and protracted issues as the cutting of the Bridgewater Canal through the estate. It was only thanks to her great tenacity that the Duke of Bridgewater did not renege on promises to protect her interests and those of the other landowners whose estates were affected by the canal.

Lady Mary had married Harry, Lord Grey of Groby, later 4th Earl of Stamford, in 1736 when he was twenty and she was at the comparatively advanced age, for then, of 32. Despite their disparity in age, the shattered relationships of both sets of parents, and the fact that this was probably an arranged marriage, they proved a contented and, as far as one can tell, loving couple. While she devoted herself to preserving Lord Warrington's house and the Old Park unaltered, and laid out the New Park, the Earl continued developing the extraordinary park at Enville, his seat in Staffordshire. Lady Stamford does not seem to have had the quarrelsome nature of her father, nor the wildness of her mother. Her daughter-in-law wrote in 1766 that her 'greatest Joy is to make those belonging to her happy and easy'. The Countess's letters and books reveal her to have been highly educated and something of a bluestocking: poetry, natural history, plays and religious topics predominate amongst the volumes bearing her bookplate.

THE GREYS

The Greys were a far more illustrious family than the Booths. They claimed descent from the chamberlain to Robert, Duke of Normandy, and had royal links through the marriage of Elizabeth Woodville, widow of Sir John Grey, 7th Lord Ferrers of Groby, and ancestress of the Earls of Stamford, to King Edward IV. Her eldest son by Lord Ferrers, Sir Thomas Grey, was advanced to the Marquessate of Dorset in 1475, and in 1533 the 3rd Marquess renewed the links with the royal family by marrying Frances Brandon, daughter of Henry VIII's sister, Mary. Lord Dorset was elevated to the Dukedom of Suffolk in 1551, and two years later the Greys reached the height of their power when his eldest daughter, Lady Jane Grey, was declared Queen on the death of Edward VI. Nine days later she was deposed, and, following the continued intriguing of her father, she, her young husband Lord Guildford Dudley, the Duke himself and her uncle, Lord Thomas Grey, were all executed, and the family estates were confiscated.

Suffolk's youngest brother, John, was the only one to escape with his life, and it was his son, Henry, who revived the family fortunes. Having already retrieved the Leicestershire estates, he was knighted by Elizabeth I in 1587 and, on the accession of James I in 1603, he was created Baron Grey of Groby. He returned to the great house at Bradgate in Leicestershire, which had been built by the 1st and 2nd Marquesses of Dorset, and the Greys remained seated there until the early 18th century. The 2nd Baron was raised to the Earldom of Stamford in 1628 and was a military commander for Parliament during the Civil War, but did not support the execution of the King, unlike his regicide eldest son, Thomas, Lord Grey of Groby. Thomas's sister, Elizabeth, made the first link between the Greys and the Booths by marrying 'Young' Sir George Booth.

The 2nd Earl of Stamford, like his cousin, the 1st Earl of Warrington, was suspected of involvement in both the Rye House Plot and the Monmouth Rebellion, and played a key role in the Glorious Revolution of 1688. On his death, childless, in 1720, the Earldom passed to his cousin, Harry Grey of Enville in Staffordshire. The 3rd Earl, according to the contemporary diarist Dr Wilkes, was made 'almost a lunatic' by drink and abused his wife, who eventually left him. He developed numerous phobias, including fancying himself injured if seen by other people, and 'made all his servants come into and go out of the room with their backs turned towards him'. But for the marriage of his son to Lady Mary Booth, Dr Wilkes (perhaps exaggeratedly) considered that the family would have been ruined by the Earl's profligacy.

THE EARLS OF STAMFORD

On the death of the Countess of Stamford in 1772, the Booth lands, including Dunham Massey, passed to her eldest son, George Harry Grey, who had already succeeded to his father's property and the Earldom. He had been named in anticipation of the union of the families and their estates – George after his Booth ancestors and Harry after the Greys – and in 1796 the Earldom of Warrington and Barony of Delamer were revived in his favour: for four generations the titles and estates remained united, and each successive heir was christened George Harry. Until the 1850s the year was divided between London, Enville

The 5th Earl (third from left) inspecting the classical monuments at Pula; by Thomas Patch (Tea Room)

The 5th Earl of Stamford; painted in Rome in 1760 by A. R. Mengs (Tea Room)

and Dunham, and, following the pattern set by the Countess of Stamford, the Earl was in Cheshire from July until late November or early December.

The 5th Earl brought in John Hope of Liverpool to remodel and enlarge Enville in 1775–80 and alter the south front of Dunham in 1789–90. Despite being brother-in-law to the 3rd Duke of Portland, who was twice Prime Minister, he generally eschewed national politics and instead devoted himself to county affairs, as well as to the meticulous management of his estates and to sporting activities, in particular racing and shooting. In 1760 he had been sent to Italy on the Grand Tour, but apart from the objects brought back from that trip, some of which are shown in the Tea Room, he does not seem to have been a particularly avid collector. Twenty-six years later, his eldest son, the future 6th Earl, followed in his footsteps, and his detailed, but somewhat emotionless, diaries reveal him to have been as interested in the English-style gardens seen in Germany *en route* as in the buildings and art collections of Italy. After inheriting, he introduced large numbers of specimen trees at Dunham and Enville, as well as shrubs, herbaceous plants and exotics, and developed the kitchen gardens at both.

The 6th Earl's career was conventionally aristocratic and very much like that of his father, whom he succeeded in the Lord Lieutenancy of Cheshire. He was much loved by his tenants and was known for his liberality towards them, paying the doctors' bills of the poor, and following the custom at Dunham by providing those on errands to the house with unlimited quantities of beef and ale. In his habits and dealings, he resembled 'a respectable country squire of the last century', according to his son-in-law, but his attitude towards his family, perhaps because of a deep reticence, was cold and hard, sometimes to the point of cruelty. He did not approve when his eldest daughter, Lady Charlotte, wanted to marry the Vicar of Bowdon, the Rev. James Law, despite his father being a wealthy bishop. When the couple were seen walking in the park in December 1820, a heated interview ensued: 'She [Lady Charlotte] declared she *would* marry Mr Law, he [Lord Stamford], that he would carry

her off to Enville immediately – she (assuming an attitude of defiance) that *she dared him to touch her (literally)* & that she was 21 & had a right to dispose of herself.'

The marriage took place, with Lord Stamford saying Lady Charlotte 'would not have a sixpence nor his forgiveness', but his resolve eventually weakened, and on his death she received the same generous bequest as her surviving sister, Lady Jane Walsh. Lady Jane's husband considered that the 6th Earl's intolerance was also at least in part responsible for the Countess's mental breakdown. He behaved little better towards his eldest son and his daughter-in-law, getting 'exceedingly cross and quite rude with her' whenever she showed anxiety about her, as it turned out, fatally ill husband: Lord Grey of Groby, who also suffered from mental illness, died in 1835 at the age of only 32.

THE 7TH AND 8TH EARLS

Given the stultifying atmosphere of the 6th Earl's household, it is not surprising that his grandson and heir, an eighteen-year-old who had lost both his parents, should have gone somewhat wild after the old peer's death at the age of 79 in 1845. Whilst he was up at Cambridge, the new Earl took as his mistress the daughter of a bedmaker, Elizabeth (Bessie) Billage, who was considerably older than him and had previously been kept by other wealthy undergraduates. In December 1848, after being thwarted by his family and guardian for over a year, he finally succeeded in marrying her. She somewhat uncomfortably took up her role as Countess, reputedly curtseying to clergymen's wives and being overpowered by 'the platoons of footmen, maidservants and gardeners' at the Earl's houses. The couple lived primarily at Enville, where huge sums were spent on the garden, but there were also visits to Dunham and Bradgate, mainly for the shooting. As a retreat from the formality of noble life, they also stayed at Hove in Sussex. It was at Hove that the Countess fell ill in September 1854, and, after being attended day and night by her devoted husband, she died on 22 October.

The 6th Earl of Stamford; painted by George Romney in 1790 (Saloon)

The family breathed a collective sigh of relief,

The 7th Earl, who lived mainly at Enville, one of the Stamfords' ancestral homes, which appears in the background (Green Silk Room)

but within a year the Earl was married again, and this time to a former bareback-rider in a circus act. Catherine Cocks was one of four sisters, all with colourful reputations. Her mother and her brother had both been in prison, and only months before the wedding she had secretly given birth to a child by a previous paramour, the Hon. Percy Feilding. The 7th Earl took his new bride to his various estates to be officially received by the tenantry, and rooms were fitted out for her in the very latest fashion at Dunham. However, the couple were given such an insulting reception in Cheshire that the Earl more or less abandoned Dunham: at the Knutsford races the ladies are said to have turned their parasols on the Countess, and at Bowdon, according to H. J. Leech:

The minister and church wardens ... being dissatisfied with the match his Lordship had made, refused to let the bells be rung. The ringers ... determined the bells should be rung, and getting into the belfry they locked

themselves in. The churchwardens thereupon broke in the door and dismissed them.

The best of the paintings and all of Lord Warrington's silver were taken to Enville over the next decade, and although the Earl assured his cousin, the Rev. Harry Grey, in 1856 that he 'never had any intention of selling Dunham' and would not break up the precious library, the house was let or left vacant from 1869, the family papers were removed, and the land around Bowdon and the New Park was sold for development. The 7th Earl did occasionally visit to shoot, but Dunham was no longer on a par with Enville, and a massive new house in exuberant 'Jacobethan' style was built at Bradgate, where the Earl had become Master of the Quorn Hunt. After he had given up the mastership in 1863, he turned his attention to the even more extravagant pastime of racing, which exhausted the estate finances to such an extent that he had to sell off large swathes of his Cheshire estates. The Earl and Countess continued to live in high style, and in 1882 the Prince of Wales visited them at Bradgate to shoot. Mrs Henry, the Countess's niece, was brought over from India to entertain the Prince, but overstepped the mark by accepting his button-hole at dinner, which reputedly infuriated her aunt.

On the 7th Earl's death in 1883, his estates passed to his widow for her life, and the trustees, acting on her behalf, made a creditable job of reversing the rapid slide into debt caused by his gambling and general extravagance. The Countess, who was of a generous disposition and popular with her tenants at Enville and Bradgate, might have been inclined to heal the rift with Dunham, but the old wound was reopened when the borough of Altrincham's governing body refused to pass a vote of condolences to her on the death of her husband, and in the face of such petty snobbery she kept away.

The re-created Earldom of Warrington became extinct with the 7th Earl, but the Stamford title passed with a generous annuity of £8,000 to his distant cousin, the Rev. Harry Grey (1812–90), a great-grandson of the 4th Earl. The future 8th Earl had been ordained in 1837 and in 1844 he had married Susan Gaydon. His excessive gambling and her adultery led to the couple separating, and in 1854 Grey was sent to South Africa with a small

The 8th Earl's children, John and Lady Mary Grey

THE 20TH CENTURY

William Grey, 9th Earl of Stamford (1850–1910) was born in Newfoundland, where his father, the Rev. William Grey, was principal of a theological college. He did not grow up with the expectation of inheriting estates and titles, and it was only after becoming heir-presumptive to his aged uncle in 1883 that he was summoned home from his post as Professor of Classics at Codrington College in Barbados to pursue a more aristocratic life. Over the next few years he travelled extensively, and when in London he devoted himself to the relief of the East End poor. After gaining his seat in the House of Lords in 1892, he spoke on matters relating to Canada and the West Indies, the problems of poverty and animal welfare. He became one of the first lay readers in the diocese of London, assisted in the selection of colonial bishops, and became involved with over 80 worthy organisations, ranging from missions and Bible societies to the National Trust, of which he was an early member.

small allowance. There he remained, and after a brief second marriage following Susan Gaydon's death in 1869, he lived with his former housekeeper, Martha Solomon, who was a Hottentot and who in 1877 gave birth to the Earl's only son, John. The couple's subsequent marriage legitimised the boy under Cape of Good Hope law, but not in England, and following Lord Stamford's death in 1890, his nephew, William Grey, succeeded to the peerage. There was, however, some doubt about whether the 7th Earl's Will entitled John Grey to an interest in the family estates, and he subsequently received a substantial capital sum from the trustees in settlement. John and his legitimate younger sister, Lady Mary Grey, both completed their education on the Continent, and he eventually settled in Worthing, married and had three children.

A 'Spy' cartoon of the 9th Earl, who brought the house back to life after the family returned to Dunham in 1906. Appropriately, this gentle and well-intentioned man was dubbed 'Good Will'

The 9th Earl and Countess with their children at the Homecoming to Dunham in 1906

On the death of the 7th Earl's widow in 1905, the estates were split, Enville passing to her niece, Bradgate to a descendant of the 7th Earl's sister, and only Dunham to the 9th Earl. Dunham Massey had not been occupied by the family for 50 years and had received only basic maintenance during that time, but the trustees were obliged to provide funds to put it in order, and Lord Stamford determined to take up residence with his wife and two young children as soon as was practicable. Under the direction of the architect Joseph Compton Hall structural repairs and alterations were undertaken, electricity and other services were introduced or renewed, and the house was generally brought up to the standards of the early 20th century, taking full advantage of the latest domestic technology. Compton Hall did not have an inspired eye for decoration, and so the pioneer furniture historian and stage designer Percy Macquoid, who was a cousin of Lady Stamford by marriage, was brought in to advise on the finishing of the interior. He created a series of rich and comfortable spaces, notable for the careful selection of each piece of furniture, the intermixing of historic fabrics, and most particularly for the inspired use of colour.

In August 1906 the family made their official return to Dunham and were received with great enthusiasm by the tenants of the estate and other local people. However, work was still going on in March 1909, when Lord Stamford started on what turned out to be the last of his regular forays abroad. Whilst in Palestine he picked up an infection from which he died in May 1910. His widow was left to manage the estate on behalf of their young son and during the First World War ran Dunham as a hospital. On the restoration of peace in 1918, shooting and house parties were held, and a house taken in London to launch the young Lord Stamford and his sister, Lady Jane Grey, in society. Lady Stamford was a somewhat formidable hostess, who wanted only the most elevated suitors for her children, which may partly explain why the 10th Earl never married. When Lady Jane chose the curate of St Margaret's, Dunham Massey, Lady Stamford did not approve, but eventually bowed to the inevitable with rather more grace than the 6th Earl had shown in similar circumstances a hundred years before.

Roger Grey, 10th Earl of Stamford (1896–1976), who had been sickly as a child, was declared unfit for active service during the First World War. However, he served as ADC to General Lloyd and in 1918–19 he was attached to the British Legation in Berne. It was probably these duties, as well as a period as Parliamentary Private Secretary to the India Secretary, Viscount Peel, that inspired Lord Stamford's lifelong interest in politics and international affairs. He was an ardent supporter of the League of Nations and being a man of strong principles, like so many of his ancestors, he demonstrated his independence of mind when in 1938, contrary to government policy, he officially received the exiled Emperor Haile Selassie of Ethiopia at Dunham Massey.

The 10th Earl (standing) with his mother and Emperor Haile Selassie, who visited Dunham in 1938

Politicians, churchmen and diplomats also came to Dunham during Lord Stamford's 65-year tenure, and he regularly attended the House of Lords, although he never spoke there. He played a prominent part in local affairs, as a magistrate and a Deputy Lieutenant for Cheshire for many years, and in 1937 he was Charter Mayor of Altrincham. Considered a model landlord, he continued to restore the estate and fought for its preservation in the face of the numerous pressures of the 20th century. He would visit his tenants and workmen on an almost daily basis; he was very fond of his family, had numerous friends locally and nationally, and regularly entertained small numbers of people to tea or lunch, as well as occasionally giving tours of the house to specialist groups. All in all, he was far from being the recluse he was sometimes considered, and he is still held in deep respect by those who knew him.

Lord Stamford's love of Dunham and passionate interest in its history led him to try to reacquire as many as possible of the works of art removed from the house by the 7th Earl in the mid-19th century. From a series of sales held at Enville in the 1920s and 1930s he purchased a substantial proportion of the 2nd Earl of Warrington's silver collection, along with numerous family portraits. Other objects have been secured since, and his policy of reacquisition is still followed today. In a final show of his determination to secure the preservation of Dunham Massey, Lord Stamford bequeathed the house, all its contents and the 3,000-acre estate to the National Trust on his death in 1976. The bequest is one of the most generous the Trust has ever received and was made with the full support of his family. The surviving children, grandchildren and great-grandchildren of Lord Stamford's sister, Lady Jane Turnbull, continue to maintain close links with the estate, and they stay regularly at the house. On these occasions, as always in the past, the blue-and-white-striped family flag is flown over the south front – 'a mere bit of bunting and yet it means such an immense amount' – as the 9th Earl put it at the 'Homecoming' in August 1906. It represents the continuation of nearly a thousand years of history, and is one of the many reminders that Dunham is very much a living estate.